Mountain Biking the High Sierra

Guide II

Mammoth Lakes and Mono County

for Dawn, Jeffrey, Christian, Michael and Sean

by Don and Réanne Douglass

Illustrations by Bill Kelsey

Photographs by Chris Lombardo

FINE EDGE PRODUCTIONS
BISHOP, CALIFORNIA

Acknowledgments

The authors wish to thank the many people who gave their help or shared knowledge to make this publication possible:

Sam and Shirley Braxton of Missoula – original partners in Bike Centennial – who rode the Bodie routes with us, Kevin Montgomery of San Diego for his help on "circumnavigating" Mono Lake, Tim Ford for his patience in checking out some foul routes, Jim King for his input and valuable assistance, Mickey McTigue and Richard Mason for setting a good pace, Bill Cockroft of Mammoth Mountain Ski Area for his consultations, Rob Dellinger and other local riders for their suggestions, Margaret Gorski, Mike Morse, Joan Benner, and Mark Harris of Inyo National Forest, Nancy Uppum of the Mono Lake Scenic Area, John McGee, Toiyabe National Forest, Russ Guinney and his staff of Bodie State Historic Park, Jacquie Phelan and other NORBA members and racers for their continuing support, Bill and Louise Kelsey for their fine illustrations and expert knowledge of this area, Angel Rodriguez of Seattle for permission to reprint his article on bike tools, and Chris and Joy Lombardo for their photography and assistance.

ISBN 0-938665-02-2
Copyright © 1987 by Fine Edge Productions
All rights reserved
No part of this work may be reproduced in any form except with written permission of the publisher.
Address requests to Fine Edge Productions, Route 2 Box 303, Bishop, California 93514
Printed in the United States of America

Foreword

Any of you who have attempted a tour of an area as vast and remote as the scenic Eastern High Sierra without the assistance of a local guide and a good topo map know the problem. Like the fabled mosquito in a nudist colony, you know what to do, but you just don't know where to *begin*. Finally we have a bike lover's guide that is *always* available on a moment's notice and doesn't need to request time off from work to go play with you. Nor does it require beer money to drive the secrets out of it. All it needs is a waterproof ziplock baggy to keep it dry while you go out and discover new and different ways to abuse your bike and your body in a Sierra thundershower.

Most of us have certain favorite routes we have tried to describe or direct people to, only to catch hell later for such lousy, inept instructions. Face it, nobody ever actually goes out and tests the route for mileage, elevation gain and other objective data. To us, "gnarly" is sufficient description for the ups and downs, and "not far" in distance terms, is close enough for jazz.

Which is why it's such a treat when someone like Don and Réanne actually come back from a good ride and *chart it!* Homework isn't much fun, but the payoffs are great when somebody else does the footwork and everyone benefits. We can't guarantee you won't get lost but your chances of a successful trip are greatly increased by studying this well researched guide.

A friend once complained that even a map in hand won't prevent one's getting lost. He'd half expected to see little dotted red lines on the ground, departing from the trailhead! Although they haven't gone to quite that extent, I'm sure you'll find the Douglasses' book invaluable for getting into and out of some of the most memorable fixes you'll ever experience! The Mammoth Lakes / Mono County region are as scenic an area as you can find. Explore it!

Don knows the Sierra as intimately as anyone. He began mountaineering in the 1950's and since then has biked, skied, backpacked and run a number of Trans-Sierra trips. Since 1981, he has held the record for doing the 220 mile John Muir Trail by foot in 117 hours. Réanne has planned and assisted in many of these adventures and uses her studies of the backcountry to provide the route descriptions with useful background and cultural information.

Keep in mind that mountain bikes are relatively new in the Eastern High Sierra and the people you encounter may be a bit surprised to share the trail with a machine. Every courtesy you extend to the other users will mean wider acceptance for the fat tire bikes and their adventuresome riders.

Alice B. Toeclips (also known as Jacquie Phelan)
National Woman's Mountain Bike Champion 1983-1986

TABLE OF CONTENTS

Acknowledgments..........2
Foreword..........3
Table of Contents..........5
Riding the High Sierra Country by Jim King..........7
Special Considerations..........11

Chapter 1 Owens Gorge / Casa Diablo Mountain..15
Petroglyph Rock and Mill Creek; Owens River Gorge;
Sherwin Grade; Casa Diablo Mountain to Chidago Canyon;
Casa Diablo Mountain to Bishop Loop
Map # 1 Owens River Gorge / Casa Diablo Mountain..........16

Chapter 2 Tom's Place / Rock Creek..........23
Sunny Slope Wagon Trail; Upper Owens River Gorge Loops;
Great Wall of Owens River Gorge; Lower Rock Creek Trail;
Rock Creek Lake / Sand Canyon Loop
Map # 2 Tom's Place / Rock Creek..........24

Chapter 3 Lake Crowley / Long Valley..........29
McGee Creek; Tobacco Flat; 4 Trees; Moran Spring to
Watterson Troughs Loop; Clover Patch to Wildrose Canyon;
Banner Ridge; Red Rock Canyon
Map # 3 Lake Crowley / Long Valley..........30
Map # 4 Watterson Canyon / Benton..........33

Chapter 4 Mammoth Lakes..........35
Panorama Dome High Trail; Blue Diamond Dome Loop;
Twin Lakes Loop; Lake Mary / Lake George Loop
Horseshoe Lake Loop; Bottomless Pit to Twin Lakes Trail;
Shady Rest to Lookout Mountain; Hot Creek; Little Antelope
Valley; Laurel Canyon Hill Climb; Mammoth Mountain Kamikaze
Map # 5 Mammoth Lakes..........36

Chapter 5 Minaret Summit / Devil's Postpile..........49
Minaret Summit to Deadman's Pass; Red's Meadow Hot Springs
Map # 6 Minaret Summit / Devil's Postpile..........50

Chapter 6 Owens River Headwaters..........53
Mammoth Scenic Loop; Big Springs Loop; Inyo Craters Loop;
Hartley Springs Campground; Obsidian Dome to Glass Creek;
Deadman Creek to June Lake
Map # 7 Owens River Headwaters..........54

Chapter 7 Glass Mountain / Pizona.................61
Big Sand Flat to Crooked Meadow; Sentinel Meadow to
Taylor Canyon; McGee Canyon to Taylor Canyon;
Sawmill Meadow Loop; Adobe Valley;
River Spring / Pizona Loop
Map # 8 Glass Mountain 62
Map # 9 Adobe Valley / Pizona..................................65

Chapter 8 Mono Lake / Mono Craters..................67
June Lake Loop; Devil's Punch Bowl; Pumice Valley
High Loop; Black Point / Mono Lake; Mono Lake
Perimeter Loop
Map # 10 June Lake / Mono Craters 68
Map # 11 Mono Lake..71

Chapter 9 Bodie 75
Bodie Road to State Historic Park; Cottonwood Canyon
to Bridgeport Canyon Loop; Geiger Grade / Aurora Canyon Loop;
Travertine Hot Springs; The Hot Spring
Map # 12 Bodie...76

Chapter 10 Bridgeport / Toiyabe National Forest..83
Virginia Lakes Road; Sinnamon Meadow Loop;
Buckeye Hot Springs Loop; Twin Lakes to Summers
Meadow Loop; Fremont-Carson Route; Rodriguez Flat
Map # 13 South Toiyabe...84
Map # 14 North Toiyabe 87

Appendix...91
National Offroad Bicycle Association Cyclists Code.........91
Tools to Take with You by Angel Rodriguez....................92
First Aid...94
References and Sources...95

Riding the High Sierra Country
Introduction to Mono County

by Jim King

My wife and I live year-round at 9700 ft. in a canyon between Bishop and Mammoth. Last year a group of friends and I got together to map out some mountain bike tours for visiting cyclists. We rated the routes "easy, moderate and strenuous." But when the time came to lead the visiting cyclists, we realized that *all* our routes were strenuous for the average mountain biker coming from sea level.

Much of the problem lies in the fact that most of Mono County is more than a mile high, and not very flat, and elevation affects everyone differently, whether you're "in shape" or not.

On a recent ride up White Mountain Peak (14,242 ft.), I had to turn around about 300 yards from the top. I felt "dingy" and extremely tired; I was actually hypoxic, but as soon as I started back down, I felt fine. A lack of sleep the night before and pushing too hard had contributed to my stupor. I've been to higher elevations in the past, but you can't alway tell how – or at what elevation – problems may occur.

If you're a visitor from sea level, it's a good idea to go easy for a day or two. Drinking copious amounts of water helps alleviate headaches. Lower gearing on your bike will help, too. (Don't be surprised to see 38 cogs on some of the local free wheels.)

Besides problems of elevation, dirt biking is more strenuous in the Eastern Sierra due to our lack of hard-packed clay roads, like those found on the Western Slope. It's true, we don't have to deal with the "bacon grease gumbo" jamming our brakes when it rains. In fact, some of the best riding occurs just *after* a good soaking thundershower, or as soon as the snow melts off when the normally soft decomposed granite (D.G.) sand is packed and firm.

This is the true land of the *Fat Tires*. If not for optimum flotation in the soft stuff, you need 'em for maximum distance between tire surface and rim when you hit rocks. I've seen too many rides take *so* much longer due to having to patch tubes pinched by an underinflated skinny tire. If you have a pair of those combination 1.5 things on your bike, give 'em to your paperboy and get youself a set of *real meats* ! We run them around here at 25 psi.

Here are a couple of tips for riding on sand. Assuming you have good rubber, you can temporarily deflate your tires to below 20 psi. Another trick is to yank up on your bars repeatedly, pulling mini-wheelies, to get your weight off the front wheel. Looks funny, but it works best on slight downhills or flats.

When you're riding in dirt where there's no vehicle traffic, there is no *wrong* side of the road; there is a *best line,* though. On many sandy roads there's a high and a low side. Try riding the high side. If a soft road has a crown in the middle with grass or rocks on it, traction will be better there. I also have a theory that the inside of a curve is usually harder packed than the outside. On washboard, the inside *is* smoother. A fast descent in sand necessitates a light front end. Beware of crossing the crown of a sandy road – do it with conviction. Sometimes the shoulder is the best place to ride, especially on those wide, washboardy, graded "freeways." Racers know about picking a line. Everyone should search it out. It makes riding more enjoyable.

Without getting into a discourse on how public lands should be used, I will say that we are riding a fine line in this neck of the woods. Pack station owners have a lot of political clout, as does the backpacking populace (that includes us, too!); mountain bikers have next to none. Most of the trails where we ride have horse or 4WD tracks. Be considerate to other trail users and yield to all stock.

You can climb to over 11,200 ft. on a lung-searing, leg-burning old mining road without switchbacks that's barely rideable. That's where I sometimes ride without toeclips, descend with my saddle lowered and appreciate a 24 tooth chain ring – 34 tooth cog combination. Anything geared higher than that (I don't care *who* you are) and you walk. It was on a descent of this trail that I learned *not* to take one hand off the bars to prevent fingers from being scraped by branches.

Eastern California might as well be a foreign country when it comes to being out there a long way from nothing, beyond the sticks, past the tules, and far from Marlboro country. Please, if only for the sake of your riding companions, don't begin a long ride if you haven't trained for it, physically and mentally. In addition, know your bike intimately and know how to use the "tools of the trade." If you have to stick out your thumb, you may be in for a *long* wait. Besides, how could you live down having to accept a ride home in the back of a pickup truck?

Tools of the Trade. What's listed below I consider bare essentials.

Chain Remover. A broken chain is the equivalent of running out of gas. Carry this tool and know how to use it. The only time I ever needed one was when I didn't have one.

Tire Pump, Spare Tube and a Patch Kit. I don't think carrying both a spare tube and a patch kit needs explaining, but I'll tell you why I do it. My tools keep poking little holes in the spare tube by rattling around in the same seat bag together, and I once discovered during a flat tire patching session that the glue in my patch kit had evaporated. Enough said?

Duct Tape. Long known to back country skiers, mountain bikers should know this also. Pull off 5 to 10 feet of the stuff, and fold it up on itself. You can use it to wrap spare spokes on your top tubes or make a boot for the inside of your tire sidewall if a hole appears.

Spoke Wrench. Spare spokes may not be necessary but this tool is a good idea if one of your rims gets tweaked badly enough to rub on the brake pads.

Swiss Army Knife. I'm naked without mine. Get one with a phillips screwdriver, instead of a corkscrew.

Other Stuff to Know about Survival in the High Country

Weather changes quickly here. Summer thunderstorms can pop up any afternoon during July and August. Although I've seen snow every month of the year, most snowfall occurs between October and May. When the storms blow in, the temperature *drops*. Don't worry much about carrying waterproof clothing, because if you ride in the rain, you are going to get *wet,* either from sweat or the clouds. Do carry a windshell and/or some type of insulation that will keep you warm when you're wet. A nylon windbreaker and a longsleeve wool or polypro cycling jersey make a great combination. If you ride in shorts, bring something to cover your knees, like a pair of wool leg warmers. Or ride in knickers during cooler months.

Food. I carry more than most folks, because I've got the metabolism of a shrew. Junk food, health food, it doesn't matter. Just make sure it's got *lots of calories!* Don't try to lose weight while you ride.

Sun Protection. Ultraviolet rays from the sun are strong at high elevation. Don't leave your sunscreen at home, no matter how tanned you are. You can get the @#$% burned out of you on an all-day ride. Sunburn tends to dehydrate you, too, leading to altitude sickness.

Sunglasses are a must to keep your eyeballs from frying. Besides they keep the bugs from splatting in your eyes.

Helmet. I think Bodfish wrote the definitive article on this subject, so I won't belabor it, but realize how long it may take to get medical help, ride accordingly, and *wear a helmet!*

Water. The climate east of the Sierra Crest is *dry.* Surface water is a precious commodity and potable water is unfortunately even more scarce these days. Figure on using about a pint of water an hour while you're riding. More, when temperatures exceed $85°$ F. When you can't carry this quota of fluids, bring along a small water filtration pump which weighs about as much as a full tall bike bottle. My introduction to these reverse osmosis units was an eight day, "spring-to-spring" tour through the desert near Death Valley. After sharing liquid replacement with the local burros and cattle for a week, none of us got sick. I'm sold on them.

Topographical Maps. A filter works only if you have a water source, and that's where the topo map comes in. Buy topo maps of the area where you plan to ride and *know how to read them*. Inquire locally about seasonal conditions. People around here are glad to share what they know of a particular spot.

A couple of years ago, on the first day of the Death Valley tour mentioned above, three of us made a dumb mistake. We left some of our topo maps at home because we thought we were familiar enough with the areas we were riding. We flipped a coin at the junction of two jeep trails on the east side of the White Mountains, and wound up in a canyon where it took us 24 hours to move about 3 miles. Ridiculous bushwacking with fully loaded touring rigs – the first and last bicycle descent of Cottonwood Canyon. We discovered later that a quick glance at the Blanco Mountain quad topo map would have saved us 23 hours of frustration. *Bring those maps along*. They weigh less than a couple of granola bars!

Note: Jim King and his wife, Sue, are owner-managers of the Rock Creek Lakes Resort and are both outdoor enthusiasts.

Special Considerations

The Guide II covers Mono County, California, a land of extremes in climate, elevation, trail and road conditions, and areas of remoteness. Good preparation will provide opportunities for pleasure. Poor preparation can bring disaster. We offer the following suggestions as a minimum guide for exploring the High Sierra by mountain bike.

1. **Courtesy.** Know and follow the NORBA Cyclists Code printed in the Appendix. Extend courtesy to all other trail users and follow the golden rule. The trails and roads in Mono County are used by fishermen, pack outfits, hunters, mine operators and hikers who all feel proprietary about the use of the trails. Mountain bikes are newcomers here.

2. **Preparations.** Plan your trip carefully by developing a check list. Know your abilities and your equipment. Prepare to be self-sufficient at all times.

3. **Mountain Conditions.** Be prepared at all times for the following conditions:
   •High elevation: Allow time for your body to acclimatize to minimize the possibility of altitude sickness. You may need 3 days or more before attempting a strenuous trip, or one at high elevation. If you have symptoms of nausea, headache, dizziness or shortness of breath, descend to a lower elevation to rest and recover.
   •Sun: Protect your skin against the sun's harmful rays. The higher you go, the more damaging the sun can become. Use sun screen with a rating of 15 or more. Wear light colored long-sleeved shirts or jerseys, and a hat with a wide brim where appropriate. Guard against heatstroke by riding in early morning or late afternoon when the sun's rays are less intense.
   •Low Humidity: Start each trip with a minimum of 4 full water bottles, or more. *Gallons* of water may not be sufficient for hot weather. Force yourself to drink, whether or not you feel thirsty. Untreated drinking water may cause Giardiasis or other diseases. Carry water from a known source, or treat it.
   •Variations in Temperature: You may be hot one moment, freezing the next. Carry extra clothing – a windbreaker, gloves, stocking cap – and use the multi-layer system so you can adjust according to conditions. Keep an eye on changing cloud and wind conditions.
   •Wind: Wind, as well as changes in weather, can deplete your calories. Sluggish or cramping muscles and low energy indicate the need for calories. Carry high-energy snack foods such as granola bars, dried fruits and nuts to maintain strength and warmth, and add clothing layers as the temperature drops, or the wind increases.
   •Know how to deal with dehydration, hypothermia, altitude sickness, sunburn or heatstroke. Be sensitive at all times to the natural environment: the land can be frightening and unforgiving. If you break down, it may take you longer to walk out than it took you to ride in! Check with your local Red Cross, Sierra Club, or mountaineering textbooks for detailed information.

See the Introduction for a more complete discussion on Eastern Sierra mountain biking.

4. **Navigation.** It's easy to get lost. Before you leave on your trip, tell someone where you're going, when you expect to return, and what to do in case you don't return on time. When you are more than six hours overdue ask them to call the Mono County Sheriff, giving full details about your vehicle and your trip plans . En route, keep track of your position on your trip map(s); record the time you arrive at a known place on the map. Use all available topo, USFS and BLM maps. *There are numerous errors in the published data of the High Sierra Regions, and you need to check and make comparisons in these data.* Use the new 7.5 series quadrangle maps as they become available. Have a plan in advance, in case you become disoriented, and as we keep repeating: *Be prepared at all times to find your own way.*

Occasionally, you may not know where you are. Be sure to look back frequently in the direction from which you came, in case you need to retrace your path. Do not be afraid to turn back when conditions change, or the going is rougher than you expected.

If you have arranged to meet someone, allow enough time. It frequently takes both parties longer to rendez-vous than expected. Meet at a road intersection which cannot be confused. (It's difficult to locate someone in a campground!) Write down instructions for both parties before you leave.

In certain cases, it may be difficult to determine which roads and trails are open to public travel. When in doubt, make local inquiries. Follow signs and leave all gates either opened or closed, as you found them, or as marked on their sign. Park off the road, even in remote areas, so you do not block possible emergency vehicles. *Avoid solo travel in remote areas.*

5. **Horses and Pack Animals.** Many of the trails in the Eastern Sierra and the Mammoth Area are used by recreational horse riders and commercial pack trains. Since you are able to travel faster on a bike, and often more quietly than a hiker can, you must be aware of stock on the trail, and make them aware of you *well in advance of the encounter.*

If you come upon stock moving *toward* you, yield the right-of-way, even when it seems inconvenient. Carry your bike to the downhill side and stand quietly, well off the trail in a spot where the animals can see you clearly. Horses and mules are not accustomed to mountain bikes and can be easily frightened by unfamiliar objects. A startled horse can cause serious injuries both to an inexperienced rider and to itself.

If you come upon stock *moving ahead of you in the same direction* , stop well behind them. Do not attempt to pass until you have alerted the riders and asked for permission. Then, pass as quietly as you can on the downhill side of the trail, well below the stock.

It is your responsibility to ensure that your encounter with stock is safe for everyone.

6. **Respect the Environment.** Minimize your impact on the natural environment. *Remember, mountain bikes are not allowed in Wilderness Areas and in certain other restricted areas.* Ask, when in doubt; you are a visitor. Leave plants and animals alone; historic and cultural sites untouched. Stay on established roads and trails, and do not enter private property. Follow posted instructions and use good common sense. Above all, don't be a "Backcountry Pioneer" whose reputation spoils the name of mountain biking for the rest of us.

7. **Control and Safety.** Control your mountain bike at all times. Guard against excessive speed. Avoid overheated rims and brakes on long or steep downhill rides. Lower your center of gravity by lowering your seat on downhills. Lower your tire pressure on rough or sandy stretches. Avoid hunting season. (Ask local sporting goods stores which areas are open to hunting.) Give "survivalists" who may be playing their own war games a wide berth. Use appropriate safety equipment, such as helmet, gloves, protective clothings, etc. Carry first aid supplies and bike tools for emergencies.
See Appendix for a list of suggested First Aid items and Tools.

Warning: The Geologic Survey 15 minute series quadrangles, USFS, BLM and other official maps are old and outdated. While they are accurate with regard to natural features, they are not, with regard to man-made features, such as trails and roads. There are many more trails and roads than show on these maps. To avoid confusion, double-check route instructions and terrain features.

The maps in this volume are designed as an aid only, to help you find the right starting points, or to interpret official maps. Carry and consult the official maps, preferably the new USGS 7.5 minute series.

The authors, illustrators, photographers and publisher accept no responsibility for inaccuracies or for damages incurred while attempting any routes listed in this book.

CHAPTER 1

OWENS GORGE / CASA DIABLO MOUNTAIN
Petroglyph Rock and Mill Creek; Owens River Gorge; Sherwin Grade; Casa Diablo Mountain to Chidago Canyon; Casa Diablo Mountain to Bishop Loop

As you leave the floor of Owens Valley and cross from Inyo into Mono County, you leave the high desert, high plateau, and start making the transition to alpine zone. The two most dominant geographic features of the area are the 700 ft. deep Owens River Gorge, so dramatically cut out of pink Biship Tuff (a porous volcanic rock) and Casa Diablo Mountain, with its prominent position half way between the Sierra Crest (14,000 ft.) to the west and the White Mountain Crest (14,000 ft.) to the east. The difference between the valley floor, at 4000 ft., and the surrounding peaks gives Owens Valley its second, and more poetic name –*Deepest Valley*.

The Volcanic Tableland, the northern headwall of Owens Valley, is rich in signs of former Indian activity and is crisscrossed by numerous dirt roads and trails left by earlier inhabitants, miners, hunters and wood cutters. The routes described below are accessible by mountain bike most of the year and are particularly pleasant in the spring and fall, except the during the short winter season when they may be covered with snow. During the summer daytime temperatures can vary from 85º to over 100º F. (depending on elevation) and sun and dehydration can cause serious problems. Avoid the midday sun, and since drinking water is scare, carry adequate supplies with you at all time. Drinking water is scarce and you should carry adequate supplies with you at all times.

Petroglyph Rock and Mill Creek   Map # 1

For an easy all-year ride, try a simple short loop from the Mill Creek turn off Highway 395 freeway, 8 miles north of Bishop.
Park your car off the road as you leave 395, and start bicycling along the dirt road to the southeast. In a short distance, you will come to a mushroom-shaped rock about 10 feet high. Observe this rock closely and notice the petroglyphs and numerous grinding holes around the base. Like all artifacts of antiquity, these are protected by law and neen the public consideration so future generations can also enjoy them. An alternative route leaves just east of here, climbs up to the plateau, and follows either the first or second powerline road to the right so as to rejoin the trail further down Mill Creek. As you come along the creek, itself, note the vegetation, the wildlife habitat and the old rock walls on the left. It doesn't take much imagination to see why the early Indians would pass this way when heading either north or south. Push on through the brush, and the trail eventually opens up again, intersecting with the Pleasant Valley Reservoir road. A short trip to the left will take you to the Pleasant Valley Campground on Owens River, a good place to make base camp when you're exploring this part of the valley. Or you may go right to Highway 395 for the short ride back to Mill Creek turnoff.

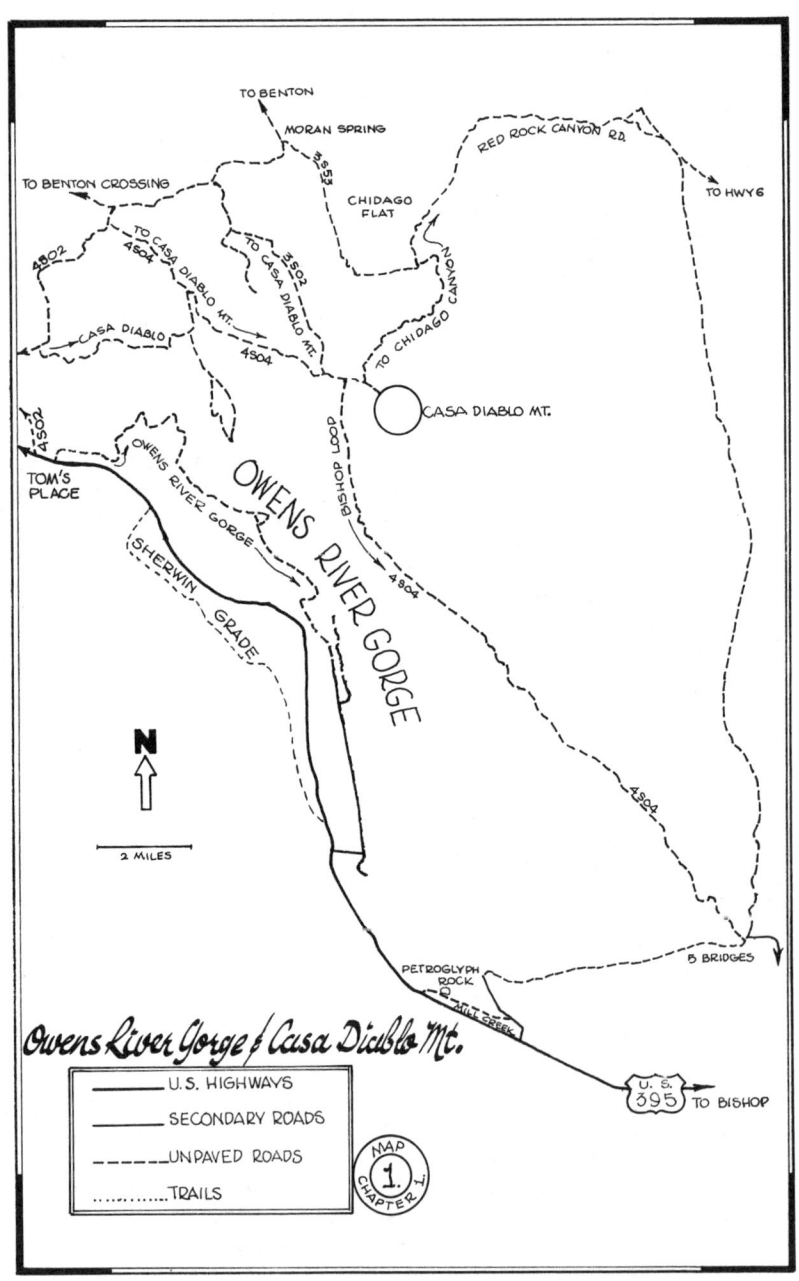

Owens River Gorge   Map # 1

This is a fine downhill, rideable most of the year except when snow covers the upper section. The many vistas of the 700 feet deep Owens Gorge are unusual and outstanding. The view of the upper Owens Valley capped on both the east and west by 14,000 ft peaks is a rare sight. Please note, the access roads to the Gorge are very confusing and the authors hope the following details will help minimize the confusion.
0.0 mi. Reset odometer and turn east off Highway 395 at Tom's Place. At the mail boxes, turn left following the main paved road (4S02) that heads north. 0.5 mi. Pass through a summer home tract and make a big curve to southeast. 0.8 mi. Continue climbing up through the homesites. 1.0 mi. Gain a shallow pass. 1.3 mi. Turn right (southwest) on a major dirt road which goes gently downhill. This is USFS road # 4S38.but it's unmarked.(Be very careful from here on; only the 7.5 min maps are close to being correct in this area) 0.0 mi. Reset the odometer to help locate the turns. 0.3 mi. Head due south. You should nowbe due west of the big house on the hilltop. 0.5 mi. Parking area and shade trees, paralleling an old telephone line. 0.7 mi. Cross tracks and continue straight ahead. 1.2 mi. Pass under the triple power line. Highway 395 is up ahead. Parallel the Highway. 1.4 mi. Turn left on 4S38, a major dirt road that heads in a northerly direction for about 3/4 mile where it turns northeast for another half mile. At this point (point 2195T on the 7.5 min. map), the road cuts abruptly south for a mile and a quarter before it turns east and runs into another road that comes in from the left. Turn right (southeast) and start downhill for 0.6 mi where the road turns easterly, heading towards the White Mountains for a short distance before it meets a road from the west, the junction of 4S05 to the north and 4S43 to the south, the main road which drops down into Owens Valley. 0.0 mi. Reset odometer at intersection of 4S05 and 4S43. 0.2 mi. Road on the left leads to the edge of the canyon. Continue down on 4S43. At 1.0 mi. you cross over the rise and are among jeffrey pine and pinyon trees. Start downhill. 1.4 mi. Pass huge cement surge tank to the left. 4S43 is the paved road to the right. From here, a little dirt road heads southeast to Owens Gorge. 1.7 mi. Divide in road. Take the left fork to primitive campsites with good views down into the Gorge. The gorge is 600 to 700 feet deep at this point, from the rim to the floor of the canyon. Continue downhill paralleling the Gorge. 1.85 mi. Paved road to the west. Go left (southeast), on the dirt road to a lookout point where there's an old cement mixer. Continue down the dirt road and pick up the paved road at mile 2.3. Turn left , heading east again, to the outlet of tunnel where the 8 ft. diameter pipe comes out of the hillside and drops steeply to the power station in the bottom of the canyon. This is a dead-end road, so backtrack to the paved road and continue on downhill. 3.2 mi. Triangular intersection of 4S43. Pass under the telephone lines and take the main road heading downhill. *Caution! single lane paved road. watch your speed and be on the look out for other traffic* Good views of Upper Owens Valley and Bishop. 4.0 mi. Dirt road to the left . Sign: *No Trespassing* goes to the Gorge . Go south and start to leave the trees. 4.5 mi. Road to the left is signed: *No Trespassing*. Cross under the high tension lines. 5.0 mi. T intersection. Take the old paved road to the left for a view of the deeply carved lower Gorge. 5.25 mi. Locked gate with turnout. Another excellent view

of the deeply carved lower Gorge. 5.5 mi. Back to the T intersection. Take the small dirt road to the left which goes southeast to the lip and curves back to the main paved road just east of the high tension lines. Continue on the paved road downhill. 6.5 mi. On the left is a large Department of Water and Power pipe. 6.6mi. Go east below the surge tank and notice the tunnel outlet and the variety of colors of the rock tailings. 8.5 mi. Sagebrush desert. More vista points to the left at this point. 8.8 mi. Paved road to the gate on the edge of the canyon. Return to road 4S43. 10.2 mi. A dirt road goes out to a promontory on the edge of the Gorge where a foot trail heads down to big elbow at the bottom of the canyon. Mileage back at the main paved road: 11.6 mi. 12.8 mi. From this point, along the 8 ft. pipe, there's a beautiful view of Round Valley, Horton Creek drainage, Upper Buttermilk and Pine Creek, with the Tungsten Hills in the foreground. (See *Mountain Biking the High Sierra, Guide I* for the description of routes in those areas.) 13.6 mi. A trail on the right goes to an old stone miner's shack. 14.0 mi. Junction with the road which leads west to Highway 395. (The road straight ahead goes into the Lower Gorge Power Station where Lower Rock Creek joins the Owens River.) There's a parking area for fishermen, and a dirt road goes a short way up the Owens River.16.7 mi. Highway 395. You may return to Tom's Place by returning to Highway 395 or by crossing the freeway and taking the old 395 past Paradise Lodge and Lower Rock Creek, rejoining the Freeway just below Tom's Place.

Sherwin Grade   Map # 1

Several jeep roads and trails lead south down Sherwin Grade between Highway 395 and the Rock Creek Gorge to the west. Most of these roads are infrequently used, and while several of them offer very good views down into the deep Rock Creek Gorge, they are somewhat difficult to find, as well as to describe adequately. If you have an adventurous bent, try any of the numerous roads leading off the south bound side of 395, starting 2 miles below Tom's Place. The power line road described below is one example of these numerous roads.

Head south on Highway 395, to the *Scenic View* sign on the west side of the road. Just after the point where the power line crosses the freeway, take the little road that sneaks off to the right. Set odometer to 0.0 mi. This route is a powerline access road recently bladed. The road bed is quite rocky but is all right for a slow descent. At 0.7 mi. there's a good vista point down into the lower Rock Creek Gorge. 1.2 mi. Cross to the west side of the power line and head towards Mt. Tom. 1.8 mi. just north of a little rock outcropping, leave your bike and walk about 150 yards due west (towards Wheeler Crest), to the edge of Rock Creek Gorge. Look directly across the gorge to the left of the large basaltic formations (which resemble those of Devil's Post Pile),and see where – in the last major earthquake – a rock avalanche covered the floor of the canyon with about 3-4 feet of rock. Farther on down the trail, you can see more evidence of rock avalanches which occurred in 1986. Continue on downhill. 2.5 mi. Cross to the east side of the power lines as you leave the pinyons. You can see the road to Paradise as it follows the east ridge of the Lower Rock Creek Gorge. From here on, the road is bumpy and there is no shade, so you need to carry water and wear sunglasses. 3.5 mi. Bear right at the fork. 4.6 mi. 5000 ft. elevation level. Stay on the newly bladed road. 5.2 mi. Y in the road.

Go left through a gate and return via Highway 395. If you take the right fork you come to a gully 30 feet deep, so it's adviseable to join 395 here. Continue down to Pine Creek Road (where there's parking for 10 cars) and return to Tom's Place via either 395 or Lower Rock Creek Road – known also as Old Sherwin Grade Road – immediately to the west.

Casa Diablo Mountain to Chidago Canyon   Map #1
Water: No sources. Carry adequate supplies (minimum of 4 pints).
Level of Difficulty: Moderate to strenuous.
Elevation: 6500 ft. to 7600 ft.

Casa Diablo Mountain dominates the high plateau above Owens Valley, an area of wind-swept juniper, pinyon, mountain mahogany and occasional stands of Jeffrey pine. Scattered willows and cottonwoods grow in the canyons and gullies, and in late spring, the plateau floor is covered with wildflowers. If you like solitude, you will enjoy miles of mountain bike riding, here, and the following description will give you just a brief introduction to the surprises awaiting you.
The most direct route to Casa Diablo Mountain, located in the middle of the volcanic tableland, due east from Tom's Place, starts at the intersection of Benton Crossing Road, which goes east from Highway 395 at Whitmore, and the Forest Service Road 4S02, the main road north of Tom's Place. As shown on Map #2, Road 4S02 crosses Crowley Lake Dam and heads north to Benton Crossing Road at the top of Watterson Canyon where the Benton Crossing Road (2S84) pavement ends. From 1/2 mile south of this intersection, a dirt road 4S04 heads in almost a straight line southeast for 6.5 miles to Casa Diablo Mountain. You may also take 3S02 (known as Casa Diablo Road), 2 1/2 miles east of the intersection (towards Moran Spring). 3S02 leaves Benton Crossing Road at Benchmark 7301, while 4S04 cuts off 4S02 at Benchmark 7554. Following either of these routes, as shown on Map #1, you head across the high undulating plateau covered with small pinyon trees and intermittant sagebrush. There are a number of primitive campsites on the little ridges you cross which offer picturesque views of Casa Diablo Mountain to the south, Mt. Tom to the southwest, and Wheeler Crest behind Tom's Place. Most of the roads in this area are now used by woodcutters and hunters, and while they are good roads for mountain bikes, they are seldom marked and tend to be confusing. The best advise is to stick with the more frequently travelled roads which head in the direction you wish to go. (Our maps are drawn from the new 7.5 min. topo maps and seem to be the best available) 3S02 and 4S04 come together, in a wide flat meadow. 4S04 turns south and goes all the way down to Bishop. Take 4S41, the short road which heads east towards the low saddle on the north side of Casa Diablo Mountain, for a visit to an typical old mining operation. Cass Diablo Mountain, itself, has a ridge of rounded granite rocks which resemble the head and back of a pre-historic dinosaur. As you approach the mine, notice the large granite wall to the left side of the jeep road with colorful tailings at its foot. Continue uphill about 100 yards where there's a major horizontal mine shaft on the right. Carved in the wooden reinforcement at the top of the shaft you can read: *Abandon hope!* On the north side of the canyon you can see the old "dump" with evidence of the miners' daily diet: condensed milk, sardines, syrup and coffee. The flat areas indicate there were several buildings here

at one time. Notice the unique wood stove with its welded chimney stack, fashioned from an old oil drum. Scattered split rocks lying on the ground show veins of ore. Look west from the mine for a good view to the northwest of Mammoth Mountain and the Minarets.
Explore carefully, here. Tunnels and supporting structures may fall or collapse at any time and injure you. Needless to say, there's no one around here to notify in case you need help quickly. You are on your own!
To continue this trip, return to the intersection of 4S41 and 4S04. You have three alternatives at this point: You can turn south on 4S04 and head downhill to Bishop (see description below); you can take the alternate loop-route back to Benton Crossing Road, as shown on Map #1; or, you can take the intimate high route following Casa Diablo Ridge to the northeast and dropping down into the Chidago Canyon / Chidago Flat area, before looping back to Tom' Place. If you elect the Chidago Canyon High Route, please note that from here it becomes even more remote and strenuous than it has been. Don't be fooled by the short mileage numbers we have logged. This route is a major undertaking! Although it makes an excellent overnight trip with primitive camping, there is no water in the area, and you must be fully prepared for survival. (See *Riding the High Country* and *Special Considerations*.)
Reset your odometer to 0.0 mi. at the junction of the Casa Diablo mine Road and 4S41, the jeep road which heads north along the base of the Casa Diablo ridge. The road is sandy, brushy and rocky. At 0.4 mi. you pass a cattle watering area and turn east, following a new jeep trail that heads steeply uphill through the rocks. 0.7 mi. As you gain the rise, you can see White Mountain and Boundary Peak to the northeast. You will have to walk your bike up this hill, but the ridge levels out at the top, and you will be riding most of the time on level or downhill ground. 1.0 mi. In the bottom of a draw, take the fork heading northeast, easy cycling now. 1.1 mi. Climb to the east, crossing a dry washy area. 1.2 mi. As you drop down the ridge into the canyon, you're heading almost directly towards Boundry Peak, the pointed, grey peak to the notheast. To the right, there's what cattlemen call a guzzler, a stagnant water container for cattle. 2.0 mi. Y in the road. For an interesting side trip, take the left road which forms a triangle to and from a prospector's shack at 2.1 mi. Just north of the shack, you can see the remains of a shaft and support structure and examine the various veins that were worked. The size of the tailings indicates that the shaft must have been quite large, either in volume or in length. *Caution: The 15 ft. opening is not well supported. Do not enter the shaft.* From the area above the tailings, you have a nice view of the Volcanic Tablelands. 2.1.mi. Return to the main road, 100 yards from the shack, heading directly east towards White Mountain Peak. 2.9 mi. The road contours north on this ridge and gains about 100 feet in elevation. You pass the beginning of a canyon to the left with faint jeep tracks. Continue straight up toward the center of this ridge and climb about 100 ft. in elevation. As you reach the top of a little knoll, look for a rock cairn with a weathered 2" x 4" jutting out of it about 75 feet to the west of the road. Leave your bike for a moment and walk to the top of the knoll where you will have one of the most spectacular views in the entire Upper Owens Valley – a true 360º panorama! Looking due south you can see Owens Valley to well below Big Pine; to the east, the Inyos; to the southwest, the Sierra from the Palisades to Mt.

Williamson; in the foreground, the entire Bishop Area and Volcanic Tableland; to the west Mt. Tom and Wheeler Crest . Looking north and northwest you can see Mammoth Mountain, the Minarets and Glass Mountain, and to the northeast, Montgomery Peak. Directly below, the deep fissure you see is Chidago Canyon. Elevation here at the top, is about 7000 ft., a high alpine desert with pinyon and sagebrush.
Mileage at the knoll is 3.1. From here, the road continues due north for a while, dropping rather steeply down towards Chidago Canyon. The first part of the road is very rocky. Be careful! Continue downhill. You will pass a power line road that heads east down-canyon at 3.35 mi. and a jeep trail that heads uphill, south, at 4.0 mi. 4.4 mi. T-intersection: Take the left fork on a well-graded road. 5.5 mi. Pass Antelope Springs, the old windmill and water tank to the south of the road, and Four Tall Trees, Private property signed: *No Hunting or Trespassing.* (Please respect the sign.) The road from here back to Benton Crossing Road is wide and well graded and, from here on, you should have no problems. From this point, depending on your time and resources, you can return west to Tom's Place via Moran Springs, and the Benton Crossing Road and 4S02. Or you can head east through Red Rock Canyon (see Chapter 3), and then back to Bishop via Fish Lake Slough or Highway 6 (see Guide 1 Owens Valley and Inyo County.)

Casa Diablo Mountain to Bishop   Map # 1

From the intersection of 4S41 and 4S04 in the wide meadow just west of Casa Diablo Mountain, (as described above), turn south on the wide well-graded road. From here, the route makes a fast, easy descent through open country with expansive views. The distance to Bishop is 19 miles and can be completed in an hour. However, frequent stops to admire the views will increase your enjoyment. From this point on, unlike the route*to* Casa Diablo Mountain, there is little in the way of side roads or confusing terrain. For the first two miles, you head directly south, passing through a shallow canyon out onto the wide alluvial fan known as the Volcanic Tableland,the northern wall of Owens Valley. *Caution: You will be dropping 3,000 ft.in elevation, so control your speed and watch for occasional sand traps and rock slabs. In addition, there is no shade of any kind on this route, and the heat can become intense as you descend.* As you drop to the Five Bridges intersection, you pass through an outcropping of Bishop tuff where you will see signs of current mining activity. You may turn right here, at Five Bridges, and take the dirt road to Pleasant Valley Campground (and from there to Highway 395 and back to Tom's Place), or you can continue 4 miles ahead into Bishop, proper. There is seldom any traffic on this route and it can be a particularly fine trip in the spring and fall seasons. Avoid the heat of mid-summer, for this is a long stretch without any water.

CHAPTER 2

TOM'S PLACE / ROCK CREEK
Sunny Slope Wagon Trail; Upper Owens River Gorge Loops; Great Wall of Owens River Gorge; Lower Rock Creek Trail; Rock Creek Lake / Sand Canyon Loop

For a simple and easy introduction to the area north and east of Tom's Place, known as Sunny Slope, you can make several short loops which take off from the junction of Highway 395 (northeast of the highway) and road #4S02. The first three loops described below use the same takeoff point.

Sunny Slope Wagon Trail   Map # 2
Water: None along the route; carry your own supply.
Level of Difficulty: easy.
Elevation: 7000 ft with 200 ft. gain and loss.

This loop follows an old wagon route through the rocks northwest of Sunny Slope, approaches Owens River Gorge, then returns on 4S02. From the starting point mentioned above, follow the main road, 4S02, around to the left. As the road cuts sharply to the southeast, approximately 1/4 mile from Highway 395, take the small paved road that heads toward the houses near the cliffs. Bear left along the ridge. The pavement peters out as you work your way around the eastern edge of a meadow, east of 395 (paralleling it for a short distance). At 1.0 mi., the road starts climbing steeply uphill and turns east, heading for a notch in the ridge. 7 mi. You top out on the ridge, start downhill heading due east and pass a major dirt crossroad. (The road to the right is a shortcut back to Tom's Place.) 1.4 mi. You come to Crowley Dam Road # 4S02. A turn left will drop you down to Crowley Lake Dam and the area on the east side of the Owens River. If you want to head back to Tom's Place turn right on the paved road, climb the hill and pass the summer home tract before dropping down and winding back to 395 and Tom's Place. This route is four miles long and will take you approximately an hour with time for sightseeing along the way.

Upper Owens River Gorge Loops   Map # 2
Water: None; carry your own supplies.
Level of Difficulty: easy.
Elevation: 7000 ft.

There are a number of short, pleasant and easy rides to the rim of the Upper Owens River Gorge in the area Sunny Slope. This is an area of gently rolling terrain, with Jeffrey pine trees scattered among outcroppings of red volcanic rock. Take road 4S02, the main paved road headed north and east. Turn right on dirt road 4S40, one mile from 395 and just beyond a shallow pass in the summer home tract. 4S40 road heads northeast straight to the Owens Gorge rim. From here, walk to the edge and enjoy the view. You may ride either up or down river along dirt roads, making

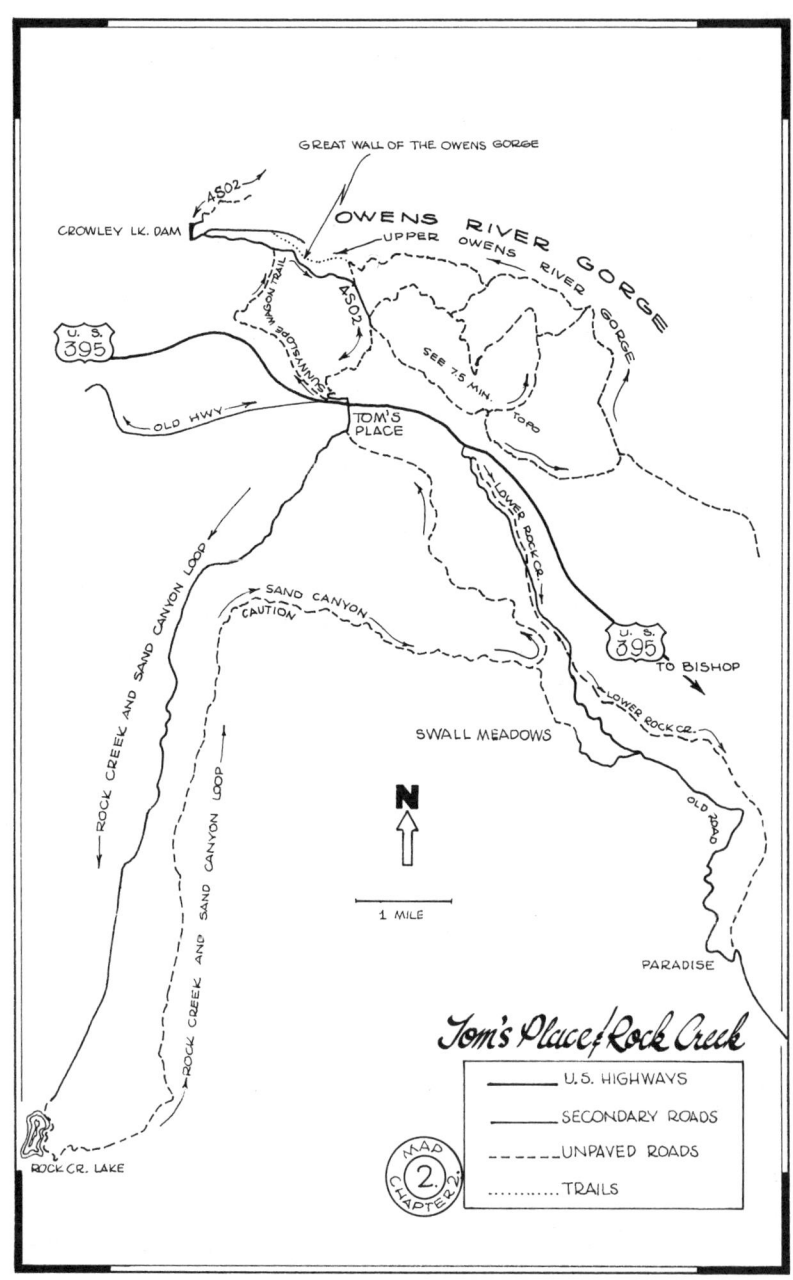

short excursions to the rim to admire the changing views. To return to 4S02 or to 395, take any road heading southwest. Allow some extra time to enjoy wandering among the outcroppings. The new 7.5 min. topo maps are the only definitive maps for this area, and Tom's Place quadrangle is for those who *must* know where they are at all times. Take a picnic lunch or a good book; there is shade amidst the quiet surroundings for those who want to get away.

Great Wall of Owens River Gorge   Map # 2
Water: None; carry a minimum of one pint.
Level of Difficulty: Easy.
Elevation: 350 ft. gain and loss from 7000 ft. starting point.

For those of you who like a mystery, this ride should arouse your curiosity. Who made this wall with such careful craftsmanship? What was its purpose? When was it done? You can ponder these and other such questions by taking a simple loop which drops to the bottom of Owens River Gorge and circles back up from just below the Crowley Lake Dam. Take 4S02 from the starting point mentioned in the first paragraph above. Approximately 1.5 miles from 395, where the paved road turns left towards Crowley Lake, take the straight dirt road that heads out to the gorge rim. When you reach the rim, look to the left for a trail which contours gently in a northwesterly direction down the canyon wall to the bottom of the gorge. This is an easygoing downhill ride, except for occasional small pine trees and brush which obstruct the trail. As you proceed carefully, notice the fine rock work which has kept the road from washing out. This example of craftsmanship appears to be done entirely by hand without modern tools or drilling equipment; precision work that has withstood the test of time and numerous earthquakes. The land, here, belongs to the Los Angeles Department of Water and Power, and perhaps with their assistance, the true story of this work of art can be discovered. With permission of the DWP and volunteer labor from those of us who are interested, this trail could be turned into a pleasant biking/hiking loop. From a vantage point above the wall, the authors have observed red-tailed hawks and golden eagles, gulls and cranes, as well as deer, rabbits and coyotes. Try this special route and let us know what you think of it. When you reach the canyon floor, proceed upriver to the Crowley Dam and keep left on the paved road which will take you back to your starting point. The round trip is 3.5 miles with an elevation loss and gain of 350 feet.

Lower Rock Creek Trail   Map # 2
Water: Carry your own supplies. Do not drink untreated creek water.
Level of Difficulty: Easy to moderate (first half). Moderate to advanced (second half).
Elevation: 7000 ft. - 5000 ft.

For a real mountain biking treat, the Lower Rock Creek Trail is hard to beat. This route follows an old fisherman and horse trail along the edge of Rock Creek as it heads south creating its own gorge of natural scenic beauty. The upper section can be navigated with easy to moderate skill and simple care. Due to the rocks and logs obstructing the trail at certain points along the route, the lower section is something of a Trials Competition requiring moderate to advanced skill. One can chose to do part or all of the trail, depending upon your level of skill and love of adventure. The paved road crosses the trail at the appropriate bail-out point. This trail, which is narrow, is used by hikers and fishermen, and you should yield to all others by stopping and dismounting if necessary. (We suggest avoiding fishing season to minimize traffic.) If you like fall colors, the aspen along the creek are magnificent in October.

To start, turn southwest off Highway 395, onto the road marked *Swall Meadow, Lower Rock Creek*, about 1/4 mile south of Tom's Place. 75 yards south of Highway 395 on the west side of the road, there is parking for four or five cars next to the sign marked: *Inyo National Forest Day Use Area Lower Rock Creek*. The trail takes off from the east side of the road between two small bolders. Head east down to Rock Creek which flows in from a culvert under Highway 395.
0.0 mi. The trail narrows around the culvert. It's best to walk your bike here. 0.2 mi. You pass a catch basin. It's sandy for the next 100 yards until you come to the side of the creek in another 0.2 of a mile. 1.5 mi. The trail narrows to handlebar width among aspen trees. 1.6 mi. This section along the creek is frequently wet and muddy, and you may have to walk your bike. 1.7 mi. Fast trail, here, but watch for rocks and logs. 2.1 mi. Dry wash. Carry your bike across. 2.2 mi. Make a hard right and drop down to the paved road. Cross the bridge to the west side of the creek and look for the trail going left about 20 yards above the bridge. Start down the west side of the creek. 2.8 mi. *Caution: felled tree.* 2.9 mi. Witcher Creek Bridge – rideable. Within 75 yards there's another stream crossing. There's no bridge at the second crossing, but you can usually cross on your bike without dismounting. 3.2 mi. High speed trail in the shade. Watch for rocky outcroppings above the stream. It's very narrow here. 3.3 mi. Parking area for about 12 cars at the paved road which crosses Rock Creek at this point.
You can bail out here; or, if you're an experienced and hearty cyclist and wish to continue down the trail, cross the road at the bridge and within 150 feet south, you'll pick up the trail down to the creek. *Caution: From here down, there are no bail out points, and only experienced cyclists should attempt this section.* 3.5 mi. Old rusty car, circa 1930. 3.8 mi. The canyon starts to narrow; watch the brush. At the very bottom of Sherwin Hill and where you see several old and rusted car bodies, turn left and cross a log bridge at 4.0 mi. *Caution: Watch the cracks between the logs!* 4.1 mi. The canyon narrows further. The creek flows over the rocks, and the trail becomes rocky for 100 yards. From here on down, the canyon is deep with sheer cliffs. *Avoid entering the canyon to the south of here in times of earthquake or volcanic activity – the trail is frequently bombarded by large bolders dislodged from above by temblors.* 4.2 mi. A large tree – about 5 1/2 feet in diameter – has been sawed through, to free the trail for passage. For fun, count the tree's rings to see how old it is. This tree can also be used as a bridge to cross the creek. 4.4 mi. The trail is blocked by a bolder half the size of a Volkswagen. During the earthquake of November 1985, the pink rocks you see in the vicinity broke off from east wall of the cliff above, tumbling clear across the creek to its west side, devastating numerous trees in its path. 4.6 mi. The 4 ft.diameter pink rock blocking the trail, here, fell in the July 1986 earthquake. If you look up the canyon wall to the east, you can see where the rock broke away. 4.8 mi. Ride to the left of a

5 ft.diameter rock obstructing the trail. Note that the old trail,(first used by the author in 1980) lies directly below the rock! 4.9 mi. Note the downed 6 ft. diameter "grandfather" tree. Look east up the canyon and notice the cabin-sized bolders that have tumbled down. 4.95 mi. There's an overhanging rock under which you can take shelter during a rain shower. Nice picnicking area along this stretch of the creek. Note the columnar rock formations in the grey band which resemble those of Devil's Post Pile. 5.1 mi. The stream which flows more gently at this point has several elbows where you'll find primitive campsites. 5.2 mi. Big erratic rocks among the trees. Nice camping here. As you leave this area, the trail curves up a scree and talus slope, and the next 100 yards are miserable. 5.3 mi. Back along the creek. 5.5 mi. Look up on the west side of the creek, 100 feet above , to locate a natural cave at the base of a vertical ledge. You could use this cave for emergency shelter to lie down and get shelter from the weather. Firewood has been stashed in the cave for emergency use. 5.8 mi. Heavy rocks from the west side cover much of the trail. Note that the trail peters out on the east side. Look for a large 6 ft. diameter tree straddling the creek, useable as a bridge. Cross to the west side of the creek and continue south. 5.9 mi. As of this writing in 1987, the trail is covered by 3 ft. of rock here. 6.4 mi. The trail is overgrown with brush. 6.5 mi. The trail opens up. 6.6 mi. Cross to the east side of the creek on a small bridge. 6.7 mi. Cross back to the west side of the creek on a small bridge. 6.8 mi. Cross back to the east side and traverse a long scree slope. 6.9 mi. Watch for a 4 ft. diameter rock in the center of a high-speed section of trail. 7.0 mi. Cross on a wide bridge to the west side again, and continue on a wide high-speed trail. 7.2 mi. Pick up a jeep trail. 7.5 mi. Cross the stream to the east. If you want to avoid a cold water crossing, you can cross 30 ft. downstream on a small foot bridge.
7.8 mi. Paradise Lodge and paved road. Return to the starting point via the paved Lower Rock Creek/Old Sherwin Grade Road on your right.

Rock Creek Lake / Sand Canyon Loop   Map # 2
Water: Carry adequate supplies: 3-4 pints. Springs which feed into Witcher Creek, on the downhill run, can be used. Treat questionable water.
Level of Difficulty: Strenuous
Elevation: 7000 ft. to 10,000 ft. and return.

For a strenuous trip covering a lot of ground over varied conditions and scenery, try this route. If you are prepared for the brutal combination of high elevation gain, thin air at high altititude, long distance and some challenging bicycle handling, this may be for you.
Starting from Tom's Place (parking space available on the old road 250 yards east of the Tom's Place store), head for Rock Creek Campground, 8 miles up the canyon via the paved road which follows Rock Creek. Just after you pass Rock Creek Lake Resort, turn left and head to the end of the road at Rock Creek Lake Campground on the east side of the lake. From here, you pick up a dirt service road for the summer cabins on the slopes a little farther south. Watch for and take the trail that leads sharply northeast (left) and contours up across an open rock face. Across the face, the trail turns more easterly and climbs up a small shallow canyon. This trail is marked as the "blue loop"(watch for the blue diamonds tacked to the trees) for

winter crosscountry skiers. As you reach a relatively flat bench at the 10,000 ft. contour, you will pick up a jeep road which starts its long 3,000 ft. descent along this bench, all the way back out of the canyon. This is a beautiful high area and is seldom visited. *Use caution befitting remote areas and do not be tempted to enter the John Muir Wilderness Areas.* Six miles north of Rock Creek Lake, the road reaches the northern extreme of Wheeler Ridge, veers sharply east and drops steeply down Sand Canyon. *Extreme caution and care are necessary.It is difficult to maintain bike control if you are tired.* Walk your bike down the one mile stretch if necessary. The road is also badly rutted by 4WD vehicles which adds to the downhill excitement! After climbing out of Sand Canyon, you pass through a fine old forest of jeffrey pine, and you once again drop down a gnarly path which challenges the best. As you come out into the open along Witcher Creek, at about 6,700 ft. elevation, take the power line road 4S54 left (north). This road winds its way to just below the Holiday Group Campground. Return as indicated on map #2 to the starting point at Tom's Place.

Note: This route may get early snow. One of the authors discovered in October several years ago that mountain bikes don't do too well when the snow covers the cranks! At any time you're travelling the backcountry of the High Sierra, keep one eye out for abrupt weather changes.

Caution:This route crosses the Sherwin Deer Migration path. In both the fall and spring, 2000 or more deer travel through these slopes. Needless to say, people feel strongly that these "natives" deserve the right-of-way and cyclists should be careful not to offend or molest these gentle creatures.

CHAPTER 3

LAKE CROWLEY / LONG VALLEY
McGee Creek; Tobacco Flat; 4 Trees; Moran Spring to Watterson Troughs Loop; Clover Patch to Wildrose Canyon; Banner Ridge; Red Rock Canyon

Old Highway 395 Map # 3

West and north of Tom's Place, Old Highway 395 is maintained as a secondary road for local traffic and is used as a route for training rides. At 7,000 ft. elevation, the good weather, pure air and beautiful scenery make this a popular ride any time of day. Old 395 heads 8 miles across Long Valley and rejoins the present Highway 395, before climbing the hill to Whitmore. Climb 500 to 1000 feet above Lake Crowley on any of the slopes listed in this chapter and you'll have the full panorama of the Long Valley Caldera, the huge basin formed more than 700,000 years ago by a violent volcanic eruption. During this eruption, ash and pumice which spewed forth, covered more than 450 square miles of territory, and carried ash as far east as Nebraska. Although the caldera is inactive now, you can still observe examples of volcanic activity in the area. (See Hot Creek and surrounding hot springs.)

McGee Creek Map # 3

0.0 mi. Take paved road 4S06 west from Old 395. Climb steeply up the moraine. 0.1 mi. Continue across the terminal moraine, making a big S-turn and following McGee Creek which flows between the two major lateral moraines. Notice the glacial action on the rocks in this area. 2.0 mi. McGee Creek Campground. There are good picnic sites along the creek. Observe the dead-end U-shaped valley ahead, much like the valleys in Switzerland. Continue up-canyon. Cross a cattle guard and pass the pack station. There are picnic sites along the creek in some shade. Note the remarkable canyons to the south with near-vertical walls and strata of green, grey and red, a jagged volcanic area. 3.5 mi. Very steep canyon. This canyon has some of the lowest snow level in the area due to its sun-free northern exposure. At the base of each chute, you can see avalanche debris and alluvial patterns where the loose rock has collected. 3.9 mi. Large parking area for twenty to thirty cars. The canyon narrows and McGee Pass Trail starts from here.

Tobacco Canyon Map # 3
Water: None; carry ample supplies.
Level of Difficulty: Strenuous.
Elevation: 6900 ft. to 9000 ft.

This route gives you a moderately strenuous workout, with very good views of the surrounding area. To start your trip, turn west off Highway 395, 1/4 mile south of the Benton Crossing Road, onto a paved road.
0.0 mi. Take the dirt pole line road south which leaves the paved road just before you cross under the double-pole line. Follow the triple pole line only.

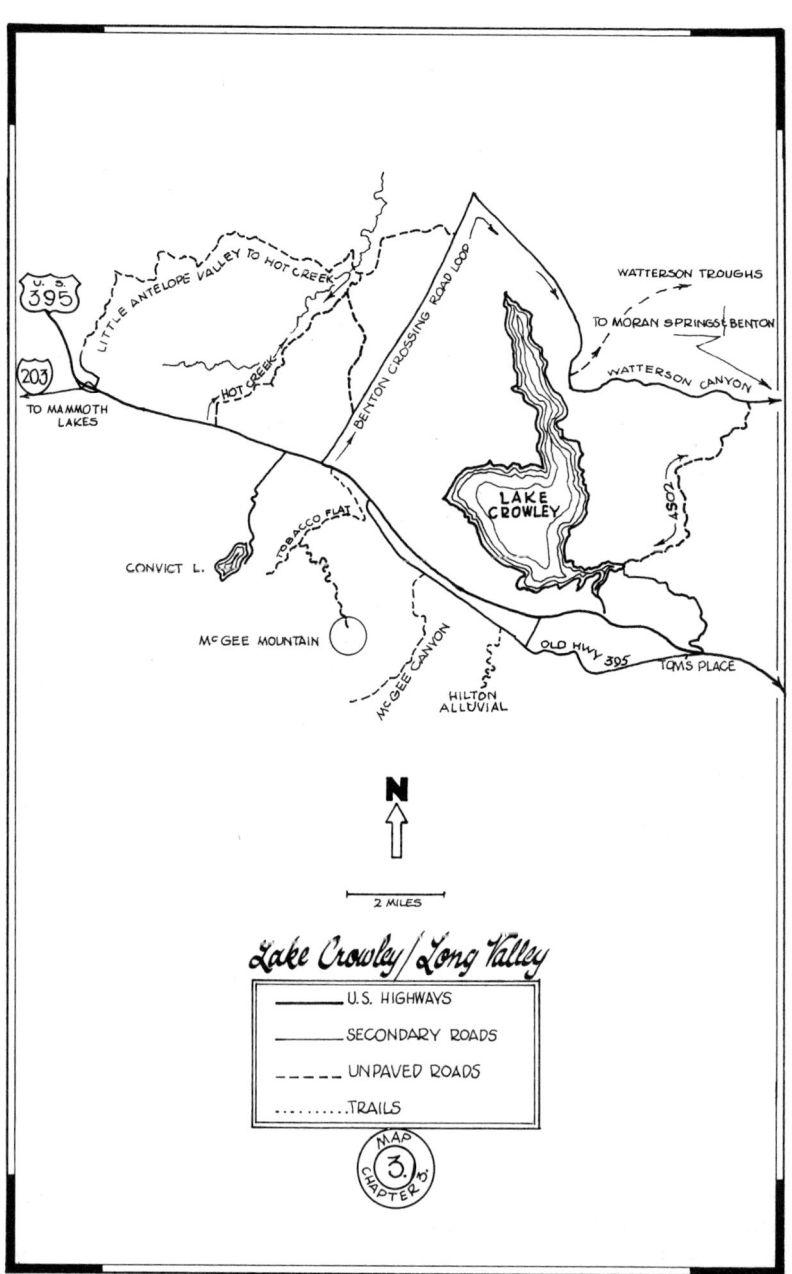

0.6 mi. The road turns right and heads up a short canyon. (Don't take this road.) Drop downhill a short way, instead, and head for the main part of the canyon. 0.9 mi. Take the second right. Stay in the gully and, at 1.5 mi., pass through a gate. 1.8 mi. The gully opens up into a wide valley. 2.5 mi. A series of switchbacks visible to the left heads to the peak. 2.7 mi. Major intersection. Take the second right to head up the canyon. (The left goes up the switchbacks.) *Note: The switchback are rocky and steep but the views east and north are spectacular. Use extreme caution. Do not enter the area west of the peak which is John Muir Wilderness.* 3.0 mi. The road contours to the right, down the center of the valley. The water troughs you see here are used by sheep in the summertime. Climb steeply to the top of a lateral moraine. 3.9 mi. Top of the ridge and primitive campsite. Walk to the edge of the ridge, enjoy the view of Convict Lake, several hundred feet below, and take note of the steep granite walls to the west. Wonderful place to hike, to explore and to enjoy the views. Return by retracing your route down the valley.

4 Trees   Map # 4

From the intersection of 4S02 and Benton Crossing Road, head due north towards the four trees on the knoll, 3 miles distant. This is a moderately strenuous route, with outstanding views of Mammoth, Crowley Lake and the Sierra Crest. There is no water available on this loop; elevation gain and loss is about 500 ft. Take the old jeep trail that meanders along the left side of the ridge. Climb the loose, sandy, steep section over the very tip of the knoll. Drop down to the intersection of Watterson Canyon Road. Go left to Lake Crowley and Benton Crossing; right to Moran Springs and Benton. At the top of the knoll there are chips of obsidian. Imagine the magnificent view the Indians had of thousands of acres and of migrating animals as they worked their points.

You can watch red-tailed hawks soaring here,as they glide, seemingly motionless,up and down along the ridge without flapping their wings, surveying the area for prey.

Moran Spring to Watterson Troughs Loop   Maps # 3 & 4

This moderately strenuous loop starts at the same place as the above route. Start to the east on Benton Crossing Road. After you turn north and pass a windmill and sheepherder camp on the left, turn left (west) at about 4.5 miles, and follow the power lines. 5.4 mi. Pass a little sheep camp to the right and continue up the canyon on the south side of the power pole. 5.9 mi. The road crosses under the power lines. Follow a narrow little canyon with boulder outcroppings and a thick stand of pinyon. 7.0 mi. Grassy area. 7.4 mi. Approaching the summit; out of deep canyon and a little easier going. 7.7 mi. Road to the right up a little canyon towards the ridge is a fine ride to Clover Patch. Continue zigzagging back and forth under the power line and you eventually break out into a hilly sagebrush area with few trees. 8.2 mi. You break out into a flat plateau with Glass Mountain visible high to the north. The jeep trail on your left goes 200 yards up to 4 Trees with its outstanding views. From here, you can look off to Mt. Tom, up Rock Creek and Crowley Lake. You can also see the starting

point at the end of the pavement, 3 miles due south. As you continue west, there are no trees now, but you have a great view of Banner and Ritter and the peaks of Yosemite to the far right. The road is a little rocky and steep until it descends the first ridge. Then, it meanders across the ridge tops, on an easy-going road. 8.7 mi. Watterson's Trough, a cattle watering area where there's a little green grass and some wild rosebushes. There's a spring here with a little trickle of water but it's totally surrounded by cattle. Continue down the middle of a dry wash. 9.2 mi. Cattle chute and a fence across the road. Sign: *Please close the gate.* 9.7 mi. Cross under a power line. Continue down the middle of the canyon on a fast sandy gravel road. 11.2 mi. Come out of the canyon onto an alluvial fan with a corral and loading chute to the left.
12.7 mi. Green gate with a road heading along the fence line towards Glass Mountain to the northeast. The latch on the green gate is broken, so you have to close it with wire. Please keep it closed because of the cattle. Continue straight down to Benton Crossing Road. Turn left, and proceed on the paved road back to the starting point, or turn right for Highway 395.

Clover Patch to Wild Rose Canyon   Map # 4
Water: None. Carry adequate supplies.
Level of Difficulty: Very strenuous.
Elevation: 7000 ft. to 9500 ft.

This is a remote and very strenuous route, which traverses some fine open ridges and deep dark canyons. It is not on the map and is advised only for those experienced in difficult cross country travel.

From the top of the Moran Spring/Watterson Troughs Loop (north side of 4 Trees), go east 1/4 mile, taking the second road left.
Reset odometer to 0.0 mi. Follow the rutted draw to the northeast.
0.7 mi. Head of the gulch. Tracks to the left intersect with Ridge Road. Head down to a small grassy meadow, just west of the trees along the ridge. Keep left around the meadow. There is a spring and a small stream in Clover Patch Meadow. 1.5 mi. Cut across Clover Patch meadow, heading for Young Teat Mountain. 1.6 mi. Guide right towards the east fork of the canyon. 2.7 mi. Heading up canyon, keep right, heading northeast, and go steeply uphill. 3.1 mi Fence. 3.7 mi. Top of ridge, looking down towards Boundary Peak. Start of Wildrose Canyon. Your route comes out the next canyon north of Wildrose Canyon. The trail (note shown on any map) heads north about 200 yards, passes an old open pit mine and drops steeply down a deep canyon. *Caution: extremely steep, rocky and remote. Suggest you walk your bicycle next 0.4 miles.* 4.1 mi. Leave gulch area. 4.2 mi. Cross creek to the south side in the willows. 4.4 mi. Meet a more permanent road. Very nice stand of aspen on the left with a primitive campsite and a spring to the northwest. Continue northeast and down canyon through cottonwoods, aspens and thick pinyon forests with campsites. 5.2 mi. Benton Crossing Road. Turn right to return to Moran Spring and Watterson Canyon on a high-speed dirt road, or left to go to Highway 120.

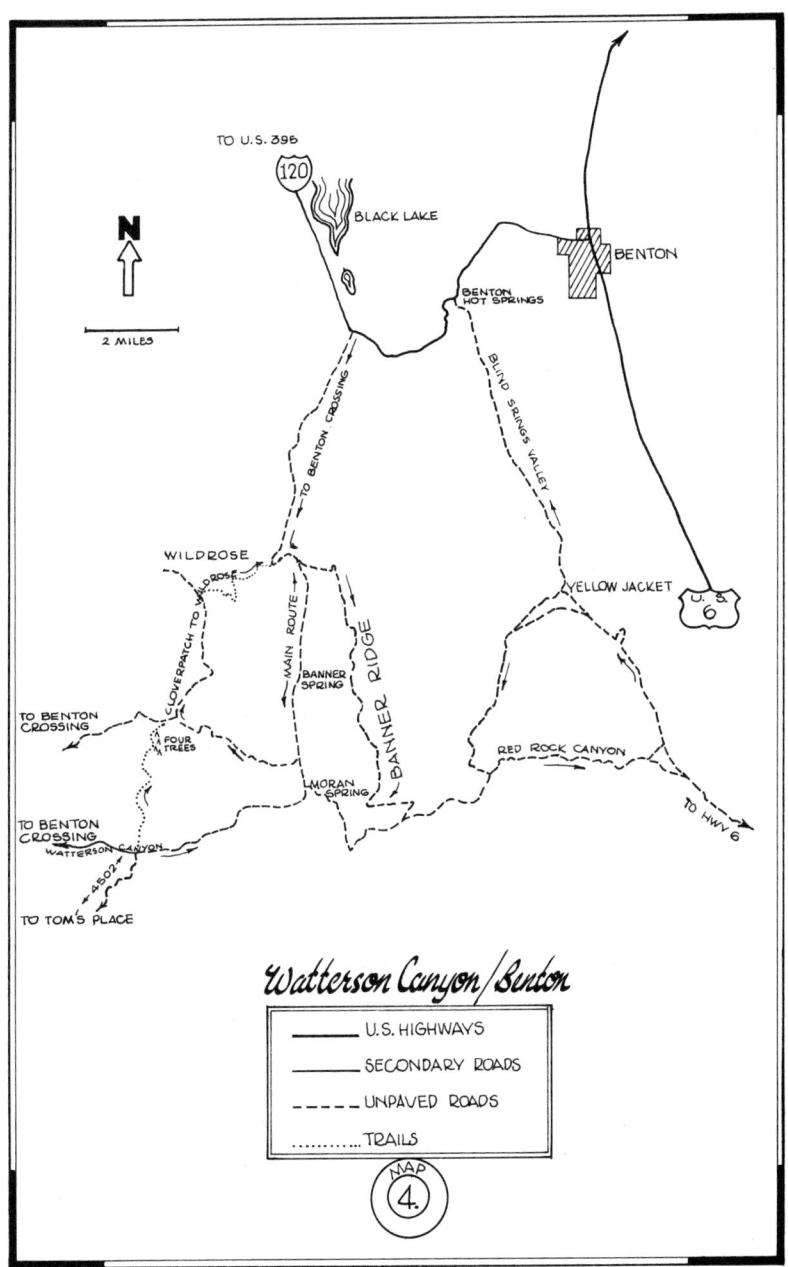

Banner Ridge   Map #4

This is an intimate route on unmaintained old mining roads. It is moderately strenuous; there is no water available, and elevation gain is less than 1000 ft. The route is highly recommended for its remoteness and its scenic qualities. Set your odometer at the junction of Highway 120 and Benton Crossing Road. Head south. 6.2 mi. Cross cattle guard at the high point of Benton Crossing Road and turn left. Cross a meadow in a southeasterly direction, continue straight ahead and climb Banner Ridge. 7.3 Road down to the left goes to a granite outcropping. Thick pinyon forest. 7.7 mi. Primitive campsite with a view. The road curves south as it contours toward a saddle on the ridge. 8.3 mi. Nice high valley. High-speed descent southbound. 10.5 mi. High meadow. High-speed cycling. Cross a valley and start to climb the other side. Road is signed: *End of county maintained road*. Climb up through a pinyon forest. Gain the ridge and start downhill. The center of the trail is brushy. Primitive campsite at this point. 11.4 mi. Drop steeply down the ridge . Unbladed 4W drive road; nice cycling. 11.7 mi. Rock cairn marks a mining claim to the right. Good view of Laurel Mountain, just south of Mammoth, to Split Mountain, south of the Palisades. Pinyon forest with primitive campsites along here. Flat spots with some fire rings. Be very careful with fires. 12.0 mi. You're following a small ridge which falls off to the east. Good views of White Mountains, due east. Cross to the western side of the ridge, heading due south. At the end of the ridge, drop steeply down for 100 yards. Walk your bike, if you feel uncomfortable. You will see Mt. Tom ahead, Laws to the southeast. 12.3 mi. If you look left toward Laws, you can see Red Rock Canyon where the gorge is. You can also see a small road down on the flats which you will intersect. 13.0 mi. Cross under the power lines (three big wooden telephone poles, and continue downhill. The road curves east parallel to the power lines heading east. 14.0 mi. 3S50. T-intersection. Road left goes to a mine. Go right (south) on a well-bladed road. 14.3 mi. Intersection of 3S50 and 3S53. Go right to Moran Spring. Chidago Canyon is straight ahead, Red Rock Canyon is to the left.

Red Rock Canyon and Yellow Jacket   Map #4

From the Benton Crossing Road, turn east at Moran Spring and follow 3S53 east to Red Rock Canyon. You can also reach Red Rock Canyon, coming east from Highway 6 (also see Guide 1, Owens Valley and Inyo County). You can ride the loop in either direction; however, we prefer to ride *down*   Red Rock Canyon. There is no shade or water on this loop and the country is remote.There are a number of surprises and we recomment this loop to strong riders for spring or fall riding. Take a topo map to help you determine the turns. You'll pass petroglyphs, mines and unusual rock formations. Keep your eyes open and enjoy the sights.

CHAPTER 4

MAMMOTH LAKES
Panorama Dome High Trail; Blue Diamond Dome Loop; Twin Lakes Loop; Lake Mary / Lake George Loop; Horseshoe Lake Loop; Bottomless Pit to Twin Lakes Trail; Shady Rest to Lookout Mountain; Hot Creek; Little Antelope Valley; Laurel Canyon Hill Climb; Mammoth Mountain Kamikaze

Services: Full services in Mammoth.
Campgrounds: Numerous in the vicinity, or primitive as noted.
Seasons: As snow permits, at higher elevations.
Water: Available at improved campgrounds.
Elevation: 7000 ft. to 9000 ft.

The Mammoth Lakes District of the Inyo National Forest is one of the most visited forest areas in the nation. *Because of heavy summer horse and stock use and the close proximity to Wilderness areas where bicycles are not allowed, it has become necessary for the Mammoth Lakes Ranger District to limit bicycle use to existing roads and designated trails only.* (See section on Horses under Special Considerations.) The following routes are open to mountain bike use at press time; however, such permission is subject to change at any time, and you should obtain the latest information at the Mammoth Lakes Ranger District Visitors' Center on Highway 203, just south of town. Your careful observations of these rules will minimize trail use conflicts and show land use managers what responsible cycling is all about.

Panorama Dome High Trail   Map # 5

This easy-to-moderate route provides a good introduction to the Mammoth Lakes area and gives you a chance to find your way around town, to learn the lay of the land and to see some of the more picturesque sights.

0.0 mi. From the corner of Main Street (Highway 203) and Old Mammoth Road in Mammoth proper, head west toward the Sierra Crest. 0.6 mi. The four-lane road drops to two lanes and the road makes a right turn, heading northwest. On your right, you see Mammoth Mountain. The Sierra Crest lies behind the Lakes Basin, directly west; the Sherwin Bowl is to the left (south). Pass Big Meadow and the golf driving range. 1.0 mi. Snow Creek Resort to the right. Stay on Old Mammoth Road. 1.5 mi. Snow Creek Athletic Club. 2.3 mi. Valentine Eastern Sierra Reserve, property of the University of California Ecological Study Area. *This is a closed area.* Please respect it. Once or twice a year visitors are allowed and it is worth visiting. Continue up into the thick fir forest. As you pass Valentine Reserve, you skirt underneath a bluff, keeping to the left at 2.5.
2.8 mi. Road sign marks end of pavement. To the right is a little dirt road signed: *Mill City Tract, private road, public trail.* Continue on the main dirt road, ahead to

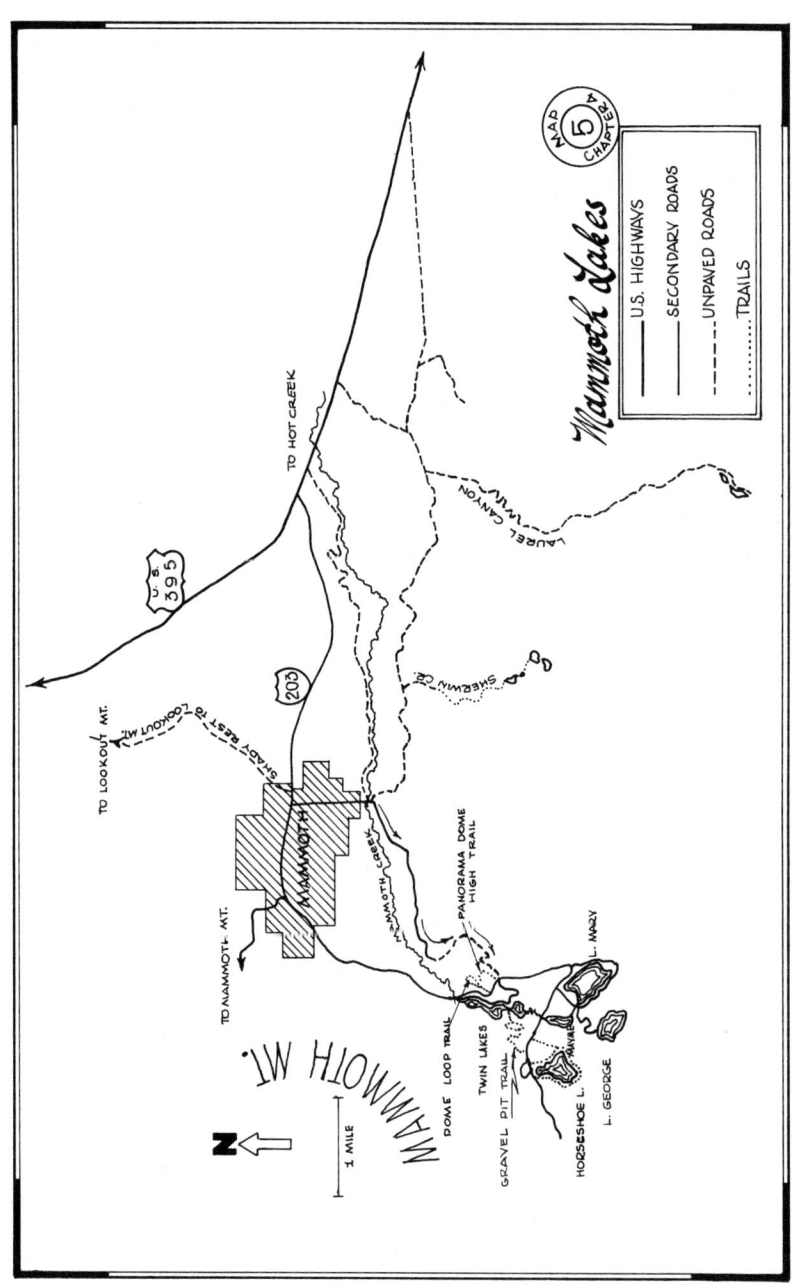

the left, and wind your way up towards the west side of Panorama Dome. 3.1 mi. Looking back to the right, you see Panorama Dome approximately 300 feet above you. 3.6 mi. Mammoth City, (Inyo National Forest Historic Site), where you'll find benches for picnicking. *On this site opposite colorful Mineral Hill, now known as Red Mountain where the Mammoth Mines are located, stood the town of Mammoth City. In this gulch during 1878-79, sprouted a mining camp of perhaps 1000 people. Mammoth City, the center of the nearby smaller camps of Pine City, Mill City and Mineral Park is said to have had twenty-two saloons, thirteen stores, two breweries, two livery stables, five restaurants, and two newspapers. Remember that a ten-foot square tent or shack plus a barrel of whiskey were all that was needed to make a "saloon." The Mammoth Mining Company shut down permanently during the severe winter of 1879-1880, causing a mass exodus of residents. A daily news report stated, "Twenty pairs of snow shoes each with a man on top left this morning."*
3.9 mi. Lake Mary Road. Directly across, are the volcanic ramparts of Mammoth Mountain, itself. Below the cliffs, you can see a natural tunnel through which intrepid skiers are said to have skied. This is the start of the Panorama Dome Trail. Take the dirt road which leads toward the water tank to your right. In approximately a hundred yards, you take the trail leading to the left which goes above the water tank and follows a little ridge, contouring slightly uphill to the east. As it approaches the south face, where there's an excellent view of the valley south of Mammoth, it curves hard north towards the very peak of the dome. This is the high point of the trail and offers a good view of the Lakes Basin, Mammoth Mountain, the area to the north, and the Sierra Crest to the west.
Bicycles are prohibited on the lower portion of this loop trail which heads down in an easterly direction, therefore *retrace your route down to the south p*ast the water tank to the paved Lake Mary Road.
At this point, you can turn right and coast downhill all the way to the starting point on Highway 203, you may head north dropping down to Twin Lakes, or you may follow the highway uphill to the south, heading into the Lakes Basin.

Blue Diamond Dome Loop   Map # 5

This is an easy, short trail loop, which passes through a deep mixed forest. Turn left (east) off Lake Mary road a short distance above the Twin Lakes Road. Set your odometer to 0.0.
0.2 mi. At the Y, it's signed: *To the left, Dome Trail; Straight ahead ,Vista Trail.*
0.5 mi. You come out of the trees and have a view of Panorama Dome to the immediate right, Mammoth Rock to the south, White Mountain to the southeast behind Lake Crowley, and Glass Mountain to the east. Continue out in the open for about 200 yards in a fir forest. At this point, the trail turns north. To keep your bearings, look for the blue diamonds in the trees about 20 feet up. The trail goes up and down gently for about 200 yards, then jogs up again. 0.6 mi. At this point, the Dome Trail comes to within 30 ft. of the Vista Trail. A sign on a fir tree to the northeast is signed, *Vista Trail [to the right] more difficult.* The Dome Trail is signed, *Easiest.* At the base of a 5 ft.diameter red fir, turn northeast. The trail has

many stumps and irregularities – use caution. Continue up a rise through a small clearing and you now have a view of the south face of Mammoth Mountain.
0.7 mi. The Dome Trail has its own loop inside the Vista Trail, remaining about 50 yards to the south as it climbs slightly through the forest back to Lake Mary Road.
0.75 mi. The trail contours due west 100 feet above the Lake Mary Road in an open area of sagebrush. Blue diamonds appear on the small white fir trees to the south of the trail. 0.8 mi. The trail peaks outs, drops back down into the mixed forest and picks up the Dome Trail which comes in from the south at a Y. Continue on down the trail until you reach the Lake Mary Road at 0.9 mi.

Twin Lakes Loop   Map # 5

0.0 mi. From the Panorama Dome, take the paved road north leading down to Twin Lakes and Tamarack Lodge. The road curves through the campground, passing Twin Lakes Store and Boat Rental and the Information Center on the left. In the middle of the campground on the north side of the store, you can take the little road heading towards the westernmost of the Twin Lakes. This road meets a road that crosses the bridge; there's also a paved bike path that goes back to Tamarack Lodge. For easy biking, this is a good area. However, watch for pedestrians and fishermen and stay on paved roads and paths.
Return to the store and at 0.6 mi. turn left and have a pleasant ride on a path which parallels the lake. 0.8 mi. Tamarack Lodge and Lakefront Restaurant. Mammoth Ski Touring Center is just to the west of Tamarack Lodge and the second wooden bridge. Cross the bridge and you come to a forest chapel. Get off your bike – do not ride – and walk to the lake's edge. Look across the lake to see the natural tunnel in the lava flows which formed the cliffs above. About 300 yards west of the lodge, you come back out to the main Lake Mary Road. From this point, there's a good view toward the Valentine Reserve, the White Mountains and Long Valley. To return to downtown Mammoth, coast downhill, staying on the main road back to Highway 203. To visit the Lakes Basin, head uphill to the south.

Lake Mary / Lake George Loop   Map # 5

This easy, paved loop will introduce you to the Lakes Basin.
From the outlet of Twin Lakes, follow the Lake Mary Road, passing the Mammoth Lakes Pack Outfit and turn left at the sign, *Lake Mary Store, Crystal Crag Lodge and Cold Water Campground.*
0.0 mi. You are at the lower end of the 4S09 loop, where the paved road around Lake Mary begins. 0.2 mi. Pass the picnic area, then Coldwater Campground, and continue straight ahead, crossing a small stream, as the road turns west. The trailhead for Duck Pass, a major artery to the western side of the Sierra, begins at Coldwater Campground. *Mountain bikes are forbidden on any of these ski, horse, or hiking trails, and violators will be cited. Remember that bicycles are also forbidden in Wilderness areas.*
During the winter, 4S09 is used as a ski trail, thus the blue diamond markers you see on the trees. Pass through a tract of summer homes before you come to the southeast end of Lake Mary where, in summer season, you can buy refreshments.

From this point, you have a good view of the upper end of the lake. The paved road continues through another home tract and works its way around the edge of the lake, heading in a northerly direction, past the Crystal Crag Lodge and cabins. In season, you may rent boats and motors here.
1.5 mi. The road forks. Cross the little bridge which continues around Lake Mary, or climb up to Lake George where there's a campground and resort.
At Lake George you have excellent photographic possibilities if you can catch the reflection of Crystal Crag – the granite tower which rises above the lake – on film. (This is the closest to which you can approach Crystal Crag by mountain bike)
To return, head back downhill, take the little bridge, and follow the road through the campground back to Lake Mary Road, resisting any temptation to use the blue diamond trail, or any of the trails leading to the John Muir Wilderness.

Horseshoe Lake Loop   Map # 5

From the outlet of 4S09 which leads to the Lake Mary Campground, continue north on the paved road to Horseshoe Lake. You will pass a horse crossing. *Be careful to give stock the right-of-way.* The road drops down slightly to the outlet of Lake Mamie and crosses a bridge at the upper end of Twin Falls, where there's an outstanding view down to Twin Lakes. Just before the falls, there's a shaded picnic area with tables. Leave the road, walk to the right and look down at Twin Lakes and the waterfall several hundred feet below. Note – looking west from the bridge – that Crystal Crag is framed in the middle of Lake Mamie, with the Sierra Crest in the background. The blue diamonds you see high on the trees designate winter ski trails used in summer as horse trails. Most of these trails are closed to bicycles because of heavy horse use.
In another half mile you come to Horseshoe Lake, elevation 8950 ft. Notice that because the lake is a reservoir its elevation changes. The wide sandy beaches that slope to the lake are used in winter by crosscountry skiers who need to practice their telemarking skills.
To find the moderately difficult trail around Horseshoe Lake, go to the far north end of the lake and stay on the dirt road that goes between the restrooms, past the sign *Horseshoe Lake, Group Campground; Organizational Camping Only.* There's nice picnicking here, and you can swim in the lake, the only one in the area where swimming is allowed. In approximately 1/4 mile, there's a division in the road and signs read: *McCloud Lake 1 kilometer right; Red Cones 5 kilometers right; Tamarack Lodge 8 kilometers [back to the southeast]; Lake Mamie 2.5 kilometers to the left.* Just beyond Group Camp 4, follow the blue diamonds which lead to a small trail. You cross several wooden bridges on your way.
Notice the height at which the blue diamonds have been tacked to the trees. In winter, these diamonds might be only 12 feet above you because of the snow; in summer, they're 20 feet above you.
As you come to the western extreme of Horseshoe Lake, the shoreline is steeper, and the trail drops down about 20 feet where it approaches the very edge of the lake
When you come to the first stream that runs all year, there is no bridge and you must cross carefully. At the northwest corner of the lake, the trail heads due south, right, through a wooded area close to the shore. *Caution: There are frequently snow*

patches in this area a good part of the year. Several paths lead through the trees in this area, but you don't have to worry about getting too far west, since you are against a hillside. You might want to carry your bike in places as you wander through the trees. From this side of the lake, you head southeasterly, staying near the shoreline until you come to the major stream that's the inlet for this meadow. You need to carry your bike carefully here. The trail then heads easterly, and the pumice soil, stabilized by pine needles, is rideable most of the time. At the extreme southern end of the lake, the trail with blue diamonds heads southerly, up and away from the lake. This route becomes wider as it continues and turns east following the blue diamonds.

Within a few hundred yards, the route becomes almost a jeep trail. At this point, you can follow a small trail through the trees to the northeast, about 50 yards from the shore. (The pumice is quite soft and makes difficult riding in places.) Or you can take the easier route which continues east on the wide trail, coming back to the pavement at Lake Mary Road.

You come out about 200 yards north of Twin Lakes Falls Bridge. From the pullout on the east side of the road, and north 50 yards, you have an unusually good view of the lakes below. You can't see the town of Mammoth from here because Panorama Dome is in the way, but you can see Glass Mountain and Boundary Peak at the northern end of the White Mountains. You can continue back north to the Horseshoe Lake parking lot, or you can take the paved road back down to Mammoth.

Bottomless Pit to Twin Lakes Trail   Map # 5

A moderately difficult and interesting downhill trail leaves the Gravel Pit (Bottomless Pit) to the east of Horseshoe Lake, skirts the summer homes and drops directly down to Upper Twin Lake.

About 200 yards below the Horseshoe Lake Parking lot; the road turns east; keep left until it ends at the Gravel Pit at 0.3 miles. Work your way across the pit on the south side and start downhill on the trail that parallels the stream bed. At about 0.4 mi. cross the stream bed to the north side and pick up the trail heading downhill which, in a short time, crosses back to the right side. From here on, the trail leaves the stream bed and contours steeply down to the southwest, using several switchbacks. *Caution the trail is narrow and steep. Keep your bike under control at all times and don't hesitate to walk it when conditions exceed your abilities.* At 0.5 a sign marks Bottomless Pit Trail. *Caution: At 0.7 mi. a large red fir has fallen and covered the trail.* Lift your bike over the trunk. The bottom of the trail at 0.8 mi. is signed, Bottomless Pit 3/4 mi. [up]. You enter the campground and cross a car bridge at 0.9 mi 1.1 mi. Twin Lakes Resort Store.

Shady Rest to Lookout Mountain   Maps # 5 & 7

In the area east of Mammoth and of Highway 395, there are a number of easy-riding dirt roads which can give you many fine hours of mountain biking. The route described below bisects some of this country and gives you an introduction to its many facets.

From Highway 203, just uphill from the Mammoth Lakes Ranger Station, turn onto 3S08, the small paved road heading northeast into the Shady Rest Campground area. One hundred yards in, there's a Y. Sign: *Old Shady Rest Campground to the left; Shady Rest Campground to the right; Pine Glen Campground 1/4 mile to the right. Fee and Information Center.* Take the Old Shady Rest Campground road straight ahead left. 0.1 mi. Continue to the old campground. 0.3 mi. Road on the left is signed: *Old Shady Rest Campground left. Shady Rest Park straight ahead. No camping next two miles.* The main road goes straight ahead. 100 yards beyond, the ski trail is marked: *Ski Trail. No skimobiles, no hikers, no dogs.* A trail with blue diamonds cuts off to the left. Cross underneath the power lines if you're on the ski trail. Continue straight ahead into *Limited Use Area: All vehicles limited to existing roads.* The blue diamond trail starts up into the hills. Continue on horizontally and go down slightly. (There's a parking area on the left but behind it, it's marked *closed area* .) Continue following the orange diamond marks in the trees. 0.6 mi. Dirt cutoff and sign: *Hwy 395, 4 miles to the left; Shady Rest Park 1/2 mile to the right; Hwy 203 , 2 1/2 miles to the right.* 3S08 now becomes a dirt and gravel road as it starts uphill. From the start of this road, you can see the Blue Diamond Ski Trail. Continue straight ahead. 0.7 mi. A little dirt trail goes off to the left, the road starts to peak and turns eastward 2.2 mi. Trail junction with 3S37 which climbs to the right (east). An unmarked road to the left goes out to an open meadow area and continues up a canyon. Follow up the right side of this canyon. 2.7 mi. 3S33 goes off along the ridge to the left. Continue northeast and drop down to the other side of this small ridge.
4.2 mi. A major intersection: 3S24 heads back left and uphill. Another road, not quite as well used, heads right and uphill and parallels 3S08 before turning east. You drop into a meadow, and at this point, you can see power lines and Highway 395 ahead. 4.3 mi. You parallel Highway 395 for 0.4 of a mile before coming to a stop sign at 395. 4.7 mi. Lookout Mountain is the peak visible about 3 miles due north.
You have several choices here: the easiest is to go north on Highway 395, several tenths of a mile, and turn right at 5.0 mi. at the sign which marks *Lookout Mtn right; Mammoth Scenic Loop left.* Cross under three high tension power lines and enter the *Limited Vehicle Use Area. (All vehicles limited to existing roads.)* Continue on the main well-graded gravel road heading northeast. 5.3 mi. The road starts switchbacking uphill and you pass timber roads leading to the right and left as you climb. 6.0 mi. Sign: *Lookout Mtn left.* Y in the road. Take 2S02 which heads uphill to the left. 6.6 mi. Good view of the mountains to the south; Mammoth comes into view to the west, and as you continue uphill, the Minarets are visible through the saddle off to the north of Mammoth Mountain. This is a good mountain bike road, but it's steep toward the top and a little sandy in places. 7.2 mi. The road levels for a short distance before continuing uphill. 8.0 mi. Welcome to the turnaround loop on Lookout Mountain 8352 ft. elevation. Isn't this a great 360 degree view? Apparently the Indians thought so too, and spent a lot of time making arrowheads here. A more appropriate name for this mountain might be Obsidian Chip Mountain, for, as you can see, the whole area seems to be composed of crushed or flaked obsidian.

The views: Looking to the south, you can see Glass Mountain with Long Valley in the foreground, the Upper Owens River Area, the White Mountains, Lake Crowley, the Crest of the Sierra from Wheeler Crest to Mammoth and north towards Yosemite, the lava formations to the northwest, and the Mono Craters to the north. Return by retracing your route, or if you're in a hurry you may elect to take the paved Scenic Loop all the way back to Mammoth from its junction at Highway 395.

Hot Creek   Maps # 5 & 3

A trip to Mammoth wouldn't be complete without   spin down to Hot Creek for a soak. From the USFS Mammoth Lakes Visitor Center, you may follow Highway 203   2.6 miles back down to Highway 395, then 2.8 miles to the Airport-Fish Hatchery Road. Or, you may take the dirt road which follows the south side of Mammoth Creek and the Sherwin Campground.
0.0 mi. Highway 395 at the Airport-Fish Hatchery turnoff heading east. 0.2 mi. Sign: *Hot Creek straight; Airport right.* 0.3 mi. Sign: *Hot Creek. Hot geyser. 3.0 miles to right.* 0.8 mi. Pavement ends; gravel road begins. 1.1 mi. Hatchery to left. Continue straight around Old Airport Road and at 1.7 mi. turn left and climb northeast. 2.5 mi. Green gate with cattle guard and sign: *Hot Creek Closed Sunset to Sunrise.* 2.7 mi. Parking area and fisherman's trail to the creek. 3.0 mi. Paved parking and clothes-changing area overlooking Hot Creek and its geysers. Park or walk your bicycle because the trail down to and along the creek is closed to bicycles. Sign: *Dangers of Hot Creek. 12 people have lost their lives in Hot Creek since 1968 and many more have been seriously injured. Some of the hazards are scalding water, broken glass, arsenic in the water, sporadic high pollution, sudden temperature changes, unpredictable eruptions, unstable ground. It is recommended that you remain on paved and wood paths and that you do not enter the water. Some of the more dangerous areas are fenced. However, new hazards are a constant threat.* **Please use extreme caution.** *In the interest of public safety Hot Creek is closed from sunset to sunrise and is completely closed from the Sunday after Thanksgiving to the end of March.*
Those who choose to ignore these dire warnings may soak in these waters at their own risk. Most people use the wide spot in the creek just below the small wooden bridge on the north side of the canyon. The authors have used this area for over 25 years, however many significant natural changes have occurred in this time span. *This is an active seismic area. Use extreme caution at all times. Never enter the water alone and without testing the temperature first. Be ready to leave quickly at the sign of any change in water temperature or flow rate. Do not visit during earthquakes or volcanic alerts.*
From here, you may retrace your route to Mammoth, or you may make a loop out of it by continuing around Doe Ridge, the little range immediately to the south.
3.5 mi. To continue the loop trip, go east, crossing a cattle guard and at 3.6 mi. passing a dirt trail to the right. Continue east over a rise where you can see Crowley Lake and Glass Mountain ahead. 4.1 mi. Green gate. For an excellent 360 degree view, take the road to the left which goes to a turnaround at the outlet of the canyon. Return to the main road at 4.3 mi. and resume heading east. 4.6 mi. Major three-way intersection with a cattle chute to the left. Turn south on the wide sandy road.

4.8 mi. A road to the left goes to a small meadow where there's a hot spring. Just below here, there are several ponds frequented by a variety of birds. Please do not disturb or pollute this area in any way! From here, the main road starts its curve west back to Highway 395.
5.3 mi. A short distance to the left is a small hot tub made and maintained by "locals." The water temperature is warm (mid 90's). *If you happen to visit the hot spring, please be sure you leave no evidence of your visit.* Once again, as this area is used and becomes a control problem for the land use managers, all of us will lose a fine, uncluttered resourse. Don't let that bad apple lose it for everyone!
From here, Highway 395 is just 2 miles west at which point you can turn right (north) to return to Mammoth, or maximize your dirt mileage by taking the turnoff west to Convict Lake, 1.5 miles north on 395, and return to Mammoth via the Sherwin Loop described below.

Little Antelope Valley   Map # 3

Start this moderately strenuous loop in front of the Mono County Sheriff's Substation on the east side of Highway 395 one mile south of Highway 203. Park clear of the operations.
0.0.mi. Cross Mammoth Creek at 0.4 miles. Follow the old 395 paved road heading north. A little dirt road comes in at 0.6 on the right and climbs uphill. 0.7 mi. Road to fuel storage area on left. Log cabin on right and some dirt trails behind the log cabin. Continue straight ahead. 1.0 mi. Mammoth Turnoff Road. Continue northwest and pass the Casa Diablo area, a big steam-generating plant and geothermal area. Sign: *Danger, No Trespassing.* You can hear the steam in the pipes and see it coming out of the ground. Some hot water runs out of the rocks to the left along the road. Diablo Springs was once a thriving resort and haven for birds with its hot springs, a small lake and a stream. When the geothermal plant began its drilling, the spring dried up. To the left, you can see what's left of the old resort.
Continue following the power lines and the paved road. A major dirt road goes off to the right at 1.4 mi. to a power sub-station. Stay on the paved road which drops down at 1.7 mi. and hits an intermediate paved road. Continue north under the two power lines almost to the point where you hit the old 395. 1.9 mi. An abrupt right angle turn. Sign: *Little Antelope Valley.* Pavement ends and the road turns to gravel. Sign: *Antelope Spring Road under Forest Service Rd. use Regulation 36CFR 261.50. Subject to Closure for public safety or due to environmental damage.* Power line roads on the left and right at 2.1 mi. Continue a gradual climb to the southeast and you come to the tree level. 2.3.mi. Little Antelope Valley, right, a major road, comes in here. 2.4 mi. Target shooting area and clearing to the right, signed: *Please do not shoot glass; take your targets with you when you leave. This is not a dump. Thank you for helping to keep our forests clean. Mammoth Sportsmen's Club.* Continue on the gravel road through the trees. The road levels off, heading northeast. Well maintained dirt road goes off at 2.5 mi. up to the cliff. 2.6 mi. Good road going down to the north as you climb up this ridge heading more easterly. As you near the top of the ridge at 2.9 mi., there's a little road that cuts off right and goes straight up the ridge. Continue heading for the summit. At the top of

the ridge there's a road coming in from the left, one heading off parallel, and one to the right at 3.2 mi. At 3.3 mi. you start a gradual descent. 3.4 mi. Pass side roads 3S60 and 3S13. 4.1 mi. You make almost a U-turn at this point, and pass two roads heading left, before you complete the U-turn at 4.5 mi. As you break out of the trees onto a hillside, there's a dirt road that heads all the way back down the valley towards the Hot Springs. (The authors have not ridden it, but it looks like a good road, with a steep downhill.) Good view here of Mt. Morrison behind Convict Lake and the whole Sherwin Bowl Area, as you cross high up on the treeless ridge. At 4.9 mi., you pass a stark white rock outcropping on the north. Continue to contour down to the east.
5.1 mi. Contour down the other side of the ridge where you have excellent views of Little Antelope Valley, with its stark white bluffs and grazing cattle. Junction is signed: *Chalk Bluffs. 2 miles.* The road continues contouring to the northeast. Antelope Valley is to the right, downhill. The road gets a little sandier,but is not quite as rocky; quite fast at this point. 6.4 mi. Road left, 3S06, goes down towards the white cliffs. Continue straight ahead and start to climb to the northeast. As you turn east, you skirt the white chalk cliffs to the north. Four-way intersection. Sign: *No trespassing. Private property. Danger. Keep out.* A road goes north at 7.1.mi. There's also a well graded road going south. Continue east. 8.0 mi. You leave the tree area and cross a cattle crossing as you come out into the upper alluvial fan and head south into a wide open area. 9.1 mi. Jeep trail to the left. Somewhat sandy road; no trees; road about 20 feet wide with some bumps. 9.3 mi. Jeep road to the right. Pass a grassy meadow to the left at 9.6. Solar transmitter at 9.9. You're now heading northeast, straight towards Glass Mountain across the valley. 10.2 mi. Antelope Springs Forest Service Road. Old corral on the right at 10.4 mi., extensive and still used. Make a sharp righthand turn (south) as you come to the major Owens Valley River Road. Sign at the junction: *Little Antelope Valley 4 miles to the left.* There's a cattle ranch just east. A creek comes in here and as you head south you're actually going against the river current. 10.9 mi. Cattle crossing, then a bridge across lower Hot Creek. A little road goes to the right just before you cross the creek. 11.2 mi. T-junction: Go right. *Owens Rivers Rd to the left.* 11.7 mi. Y in the road. (See Hot Creek route above.) Righthand road goes back to Hot Creek, the Airport and thence to Mammoth. The road to the left, well-graded, 20-30 ft. wide, goes to Whitmore and Highway 395, connecting just below the Convict Lake turnoff.

Laurel Canyon Hill Climb   Map # 5

This is a very strenuous climb and descent. Laurel Canyon is a fine example of a hanging valley and alpine environment which can make the trip worthwhile for the hearty.
0.0 mi. From Sherwin Creek Campground, head east ,then turn south on Laurel Canyon Road at 2.0 mi. Sign: *Road infrequently maintained.*
3.0 mi. Very steep 4 W drive road. 3.2 mi. Pass a hut . Good views in all directions. 3.4 mi. Road divides. Your choice – they come together shortly. 4.0 mi. First meadow with stream. 6.4 mi. Trailhead to Edith and Genevieve Lakes; barely a road at this point. 6.5 mi. Snow frequently covers the road at this point

about 200 yards from the top. 6.6 mi. Top of the road. On the west side, large rocks block the road, and a short distance farther the Wilderness Area begins. From the road, you can zigzag down the few hundred feet to Laurel Lake. The best camping spots are on the bluff overlooking the lake inlet to the southwest. This area is rugged and starkly beautiful. Notice the area within the last tenth of a mile of the road's end where, in early 1986, an avalanche carried trees down to the stream below. You have an excellent view of Mono Craters to the north and Long Valley to the south. The road is barely rideable at this point, even with a 4W drive, due to loose rock, steepness and high elevation. Notice the brightly colored grey rock due east mid-canyon on the ridge with orange bands above and below. Dramatic geology!

Laurel Lake is very close to timberline, so this trip can provide an excellent alpine experience, not often possible by bicycle. Drop down a short way and look north. Notice the classic U-shaped valley which fits John Muir's description of glacier-cut canyons found in the High Sierra.

The road follows down the east side of the canyon, and on the left, you'll find a good example of a lateral moraine, about 200 feet high. From a mile below the end of the road to the top along the meadow, the road becomes very rocky, but it's worth the view, and in autumn, it's especially striking when the aspen turn orange and gold. 8.7 mi. Turnoff to a campsite in a grove of aspen. At the north end of the hanging canyon, you'll find a nice stand of gnarled aspen carved with initials and dates which go back over fifty years. 9.0 mi. Cross the cattle guard. The stream becomes a creek and starts its fall into the valley below. The road climbs slightly to the east and starts down the side canyon to the east. 10.8 mi. Back on main road. *Caution: This descent is steep and tricky on a bike. Walk your bike as a safety measure whenever you feel uncomfortable with the steepness, or when loss of control is imminent.*

Mammoth Mountain Kamikaze   Map #7

Mammoth Mountain Ski Area hosted the first-ever Kamikaze Mountain Bike Race in 1985, under permit from the Inyo National Forest. (Plumline and the authors were the sponsors and race directors.) This unusual and outstanding event is fast becoming a major annual classic with plans for international competition. During this event, Mammoth Mountain Ski Area lifts participants and their bikes by gondola to the very peak of Mammoth Mountain (11,053 ft.). The fast downhill route follows a service road in a wide arc to the north, ending 2000 ft. below at the Main Lodge – a run of four miles. Call Mammoth Mountain Ski Area for current information on dates and practice run availability. In 1986, race director, Bill Cockroft, added an all-dirt road endurance race of impressive proportions and scenic value. This route starts and finishes at the Main Ski Lodge and follows the course as shown on Map #7. Future races may follow different courses and inquiries should be made directly to Bill Cockroft at the Mammoth Mountain Ski Area (619) 934-2571.

CHAPTER 5

MINARET SUMMIT / DEVIL'S POSTPILE
Minaret Summit to Deadman's Pass; Red's Meadow Hot Springs

Services: *Full services in Mammoth; store and cafe in Red's Meadow.*
Campgrounds: *Agnew Meadow; Red's Meadow*
Seasons: *Summer only.*

The headwaters of the middle fork of the San Joaquin River from Agnew Meadows to Red's Meadow, including Devil's Post Pile National Monument, form one of the most accessible and heavily used areas of the High Sierra. You can enjoy the most outstanding geological formations, waterfalls, wildflower displays, hot springs, and high alpine scenery of the Minarets, the Ritter Range and the Sierra Crest.

Because of its heavy use, vehicle travel is highly restricted – a shuttle bus is available from the Mammoth Mountain Ski Area Lodge to Red's Meadow – and those wishing to explore this wonderful area by independent means may find a mountain bike very useful. *Caution: Bikes may not leave the roads once you are west of Minaret Summit. Under no circumstance may you take your bike on trails leading to the Wilderness, Devil's Post Pile, or Rainbow Falls.* You will be cited. If in doubt, ask at the local Ranger Station, first.

If you are camping in the valley, a mountain bike is a good way to visit the Red's Meadow Store at the southern end of the road. The public mineral baths at Red's Meadow Hot Springs are well worth a visit. The tub baths and showers may be reached by road just above the Red's Meadow Campground.

If you ride in from the east side of the crest, watch the steep, narrow road down to the valley floor. *Use extreme caution. It's easy to get going too fast and vehicles will not be expecting bicycles on such a road. Watch for, and stay clear, of shuttle buses.* You can park your car in front of the Main Lodge at Mammoth Mountain Ski Area, 2.3 miles east of Minaret Summit.

One of the best mountain views in the entire country is from the Sierra Crest 3 miles north of Minaret Summit at Deadman's Pass. This is a strenuous trip because of the high elevation, but well worth it, even if you end up walking a good part of the way uphill.

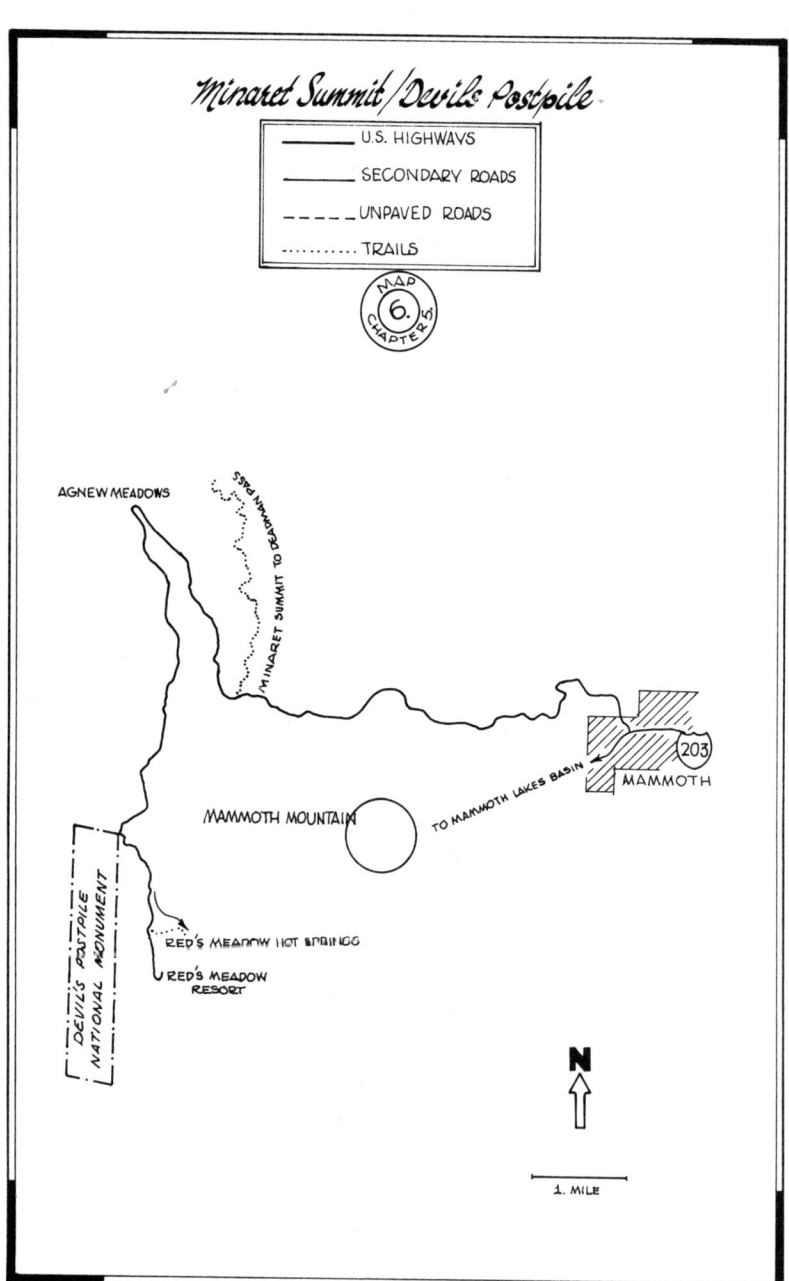

Minaret Summit to Deadman's Pass   Map #6
Water: None; carry adequate supplies.
Level of Difficulty: strenuous.
Elevation: 9200 ft. to 11,000 ft.

Take the turn north at the peak of Highway 203 where it crosses the Sierra Crest towards the Minaret Vista Summit, at 9265 ft. This overlook is on the Sierra Crest and many landmarks are identified on a plaque at the parking area.

The jeep trail to Deadman's Pass turns to the northeast just after leaving Highway 203.

0.0 mi. Parking room for about a dozen cars off the road where this dirt road starts.
0.6 mi. Rocky trail before opening into a grassy area. Cross the broad saddle through a stand of short fir trees, staying fairly close to the ridge which heads north along the Sierra Crest. 2.1 mi. A steep climb to the top of the ridge. The next mountain to the north is Two Teats Mountain which forms the north end of Deadman's Pass. Note that you are above treeline now and at approximately the same elevation as the 11,053 ft. summit of Mammoth Mountain. The view from here is truly unique. Due west, the Ritter Range with the Minarets look close enough to touch. The granite peaks of Yosemite National Park are in full view across Donahue Pass to the north. Mono Lake Basin and its Mono and Inyo Craters are directly below you to the northeast; farther south Nevada, the Whites and the Inyo Mountains. To the south you see Mammoth Mountain and the entire spine of the Sierra Crest.

2.5 mi. You reach the peak where the road ends. *Do not proceed beyond this point.* A small trail drops steeply down 200 feet to Deadman's Pass and the upper bowl of Owens River. From there it climbs up the west side of Two Teats. From Two Teats there is a true 360 degree view. If the weather is not too cold or blustery for you to enjoy the scenery, consider yourself fortunate. Note the plateau below to the southeast has several dirt roads with good cycling including some shade among small pines.

To return to Minaret Summit, retrace your route to the south. 3.0 mi. You may take one of the jeep roads to the east to explore the plateau on the east side of the ridge. 4.0 mi. Back on Highway 203 at Minaret Summit.

CHAPTER 6

OWENS RIVER HEADWATERS
Mammoth Scenic Loop; Big Springs Loop; Inyo Craters Loop; Hartley Springs Campground; Obsidian Dome to Glass Creek; Deadman Creek to June Lake

Mammoth Scenic Loop to Highway 395   Map # 7

An important jumping off point to several loop tours and to mountain bike practice areas is the Mammoth Scenic Loop, the alternate paved route leading out of town to the north. It is a relatively easy trip, unless you're not accustomed to the elevation. To locate some of the opportunities found on map # 7, we offer the following mileages for reference: Head north out of Mammoth on Highway 203 towards Mammoth Mountain Main Lodge. Turn east, cycling uphill on paved road 3S23, about 2 miles north of downtown Mammoth.
Reset your odometer to 0.0 mi. At 1.7 mi., you reach the summit and head more easterly. 2.4 mi. Pass Inyo Craters Road to the left (the start of the Inyo Crater Loop). 3.4 mi. Pass a good dirt road to the left. 3.5 mi. Pass another dirt road to the left. 3.6. mi. Pass a dirt road to the right. 4.3 mi. Dirt road crosses; steep downhill. 4.6 mi. Pass a dirt road to the left. 4.8 mi. Good parking area. 5.3 mi. Pass a road to the north. 5.5 mi. Pass a road to the right. 6.5 mi. Junction of Highway 395. You may return by taking the dirt road to the right which heads back to Shady Rest, follow 395 south to Highway 203, cross to the many dirt roads to the east of 395 or turn north and enter the Deadman Creek area farther north.

Big Springs Loop   Map # 7

Big Springs Campground is located 2 1/2 miles east of Highway 395 on the Owens River Road. This is an easy, pleasant, introductory ride with plenty of parking and fresh spring water at the starting point. To reach the springs, cross through the center of the campground and carefully climb down to the stream bed where the water pours out directly out of the lava formation like an open fire hydrant.
0.0 mi. Big Springs Campground. Cycle west on Owens River Road toward Highway 395. 0.4 mi. A dirt road leaves the pavement at the top of the crest and drops down to an old, partially paved road which heads southwest.
From here, you contour down a small, pleasant valley. The road is not maintained,and is single lane most of the time, with many pot holes.
1.4 mi. Cross a sagebrush meadow. 2.6 mi. An area of big trees and shady spots for resting or for picnicking. 3.0.mi. Well graded dirt road on the left connects the route leading to Lookout Mountain, an excellent vista point less than an airline mile east of you. 3.3 mi. Here you may turn right onto Highway 395 for the short return to Big Springs, or go left (south) and continue on a dirt road for a short distance under the triple power lines, before returning to Highway 395. From Highway 395, you can return north and then east on the paved Owens River Road to the starting point at Big Springs Campground, or you can continue to Mammoth via the Scenic

53

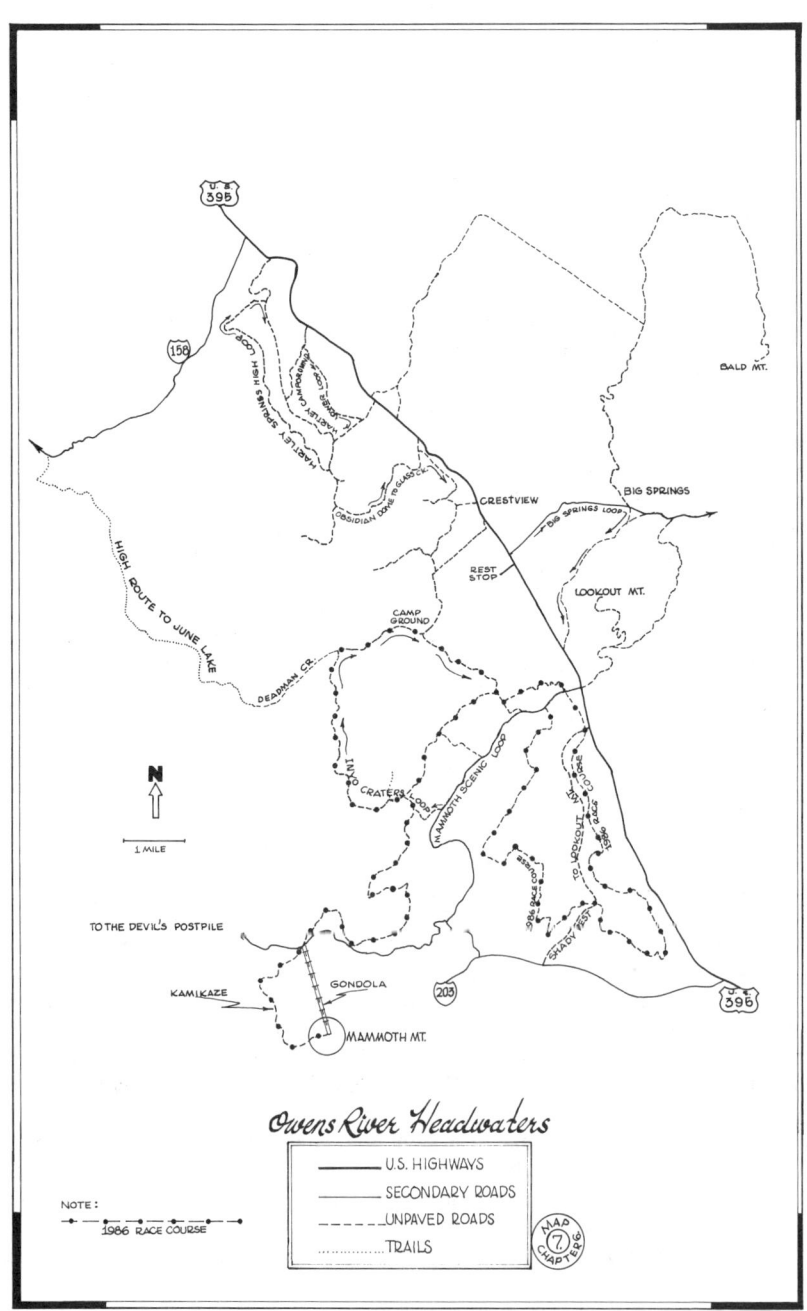

Loop as noted above. If you have the time, try the short moderately strenuous climb to Lookout Mountain (8352 ft.) to the east for a commanding view of this entire area.

For an all-dirt route of moderate difficulty, return to Big Springs by circling Lookout Mountain. Headeast on Lookout Mountain Road, take road 2S08 north until you contour down to the Owens Valley floor, 100 yards west of the Alper-Owens Ranch turnoff. Turn left on Owens River Road, and a short 3/4 mile climb to the west will bring you back to Big Springs Campground.

Inyo Craters Loop   Map # 7

A fine mountain bike tour of moderate difficulty but almost ideal proportions is the Inyo Craters Loop which starts in the Dry Creek Drainage from Mammoth Mountain, heads north contouring west of Into Craters, and proceeds down Deadman Creek before crossing south to the starting point.
From the Mammoth Scenic Loop, (see route above), head to the Inyo Craters by following either dirt road 3S22 from the east or from the south on 3S30 which leads into a short section of 3S29. At the intersection of 3S22 and 3S29, take the short road to the northeast – road 3S27 – which terminates in a parking lot at the foot of Inyo Crater. In either case, you are less than 2 miles from the Scenic Loop, unless, of course, you get lost a few times, as we have on occasion! From the parking lot, follow the sign indicating the Inyo Craters, then hike to the edge of the crater on a self-guided trail, 1/4 mile up. A small lake, about 300 feet down from the rim of the crater, fills several acres and is an unusual feature of the craters in this region, most of which are dry.
These craters are one of the youngest features, probably less than 1500 years old, on a belt of old volcanoes, extending from Mono Lake to Mammoth Mountain. They were formed by violent explosions of volcanic gas which hurled more than five million tons of rock and debris into the surrounding terrain. The uppermost 30 to 40 feet of the northwest wall of the south crater is composed of this debris. The debris shows distinct horizontal beds and rests on a layer of white pumice a few feet thick. This is the same layer of pumice which elsewhere in this region blankets the surface. This relationship shows the craters are younger than the pumice. The pumice rests on a thick layer of reddish ash which overlies dark grey massive lava and andesite.
To take the Inyo Craters Loop trip, return on 3S27 to the major intersection. Reset your odometer to 0.0 mi., and head west on 3S22. 0.6 mi. This is Crater Flat, a large meadow with a view of Mammoth Mountain to the southwest. The preferred route is through the lodgepole pines to the left side of the meadow. 1.1 mi. Road divides. Stay right, along the ledge of the crater. There are no trees in this area but you have a good view of Deadman Pass and the Sierra Crest. 2.1mi. You regain the other fork, head steeply downhill and continue through the trees.   2.6 mi. Intersection. Keep right. 3.0 mi. Slow going, now, as the road bed gets bumpy and gravelly. Notice the lava flow to your right and the Sierra Crest to your left. 3.4 mi. Cross the stream and keep left. There is a meadow downstream on the north side of the stream. 4.0 mi. Second stream crossing at Deadman Creek. *Be careful! It can be deep.*   The road to your left leads to the Upper Deadman area (described

below). Head downstream on the road, passing a dome on your left. 4.5 mi. The road widens now and is well graded. Continue straight ahead. 5.0 mi. A major intersection. North leads to Upper Deadman Campground with 18 campsites and picnic tables. Continue east, crossing a stream with Lower Deadman Campground to your right (south). Stay on the 30 ft. wide road until mile 5.8, at which time you turn right onto dirt road 2S29, and head south,.remaining on 2S29 all the way. To prevent getting lost we offer the following details: 100 yards beyond mile 5.8, go left downhill. 6.6 mi. Jeep trail to the right. 7.2 mi. Snow depth gage. 7.4 mi. Jeep trail to the right . 7.5 mi. Jeep trail to the left. Bear right on the road more frequently travelled. 7.6 mi. Continue straight ahead. 8.1 mi. Road to your left. Cross a stream and you come out on 3S23, the paved Mammoth Scenic Loop. (Note that this road, like so many others, is unmarked.) If you want, you can turned right onto road 2S29D, approximately 1 mile before returning to the Scenic Loop which takes you back to the vicinity of Inyo Craters and the parking lot at the start of this loop.

Note: Many of these jeep roads are used in different combinations at the Annual Mammoth Mountain Bike Race.

To return directly to the Mammoth Mountain Main Lodge on dirt roads, from the Inyo Craters you can use the following route: Junction of 3S22 and 3S29, reset odometer to 0.0 mi. Turn onto 3S23, leaving 3S30. At 0.7 mi. there is a divide in the road. 3S30 goes right. Take the left branch 3S89 and begin climbing. 1.1 mi. Road divides again. Take the right hand road which is slightly higher. 1.6 mi. Cross to the south side of the creek, continue through a lodgepole forest. 2.2 mi. Climb and cross the stream. 2.7 mi. Sharp U turn. At 3.2 mi., the road peters out and you pick up the telephone road. 3.4 mi. Turn right and climb 0.1 mile to Highway 203, just south of a big power station. The Main Lodge is 1.4 miles to the west. *Please note: for actual race courses, contact race officials.* This will give you an idea of the challenges of this interesting area.

Hartley Springs Campground Lower Loop   Map #7
Water: At the campgrounds.
Level of Difficulty: Easy.
Elevation: 8000 ft. to 8400 ft.

0.3 mi. beyond Deadman's Summit, turn west off Highway 395 onto Glass Flow Road (signed). Reset to 0.0.mi. on 2S10, a well-graded dirt road, which heads due west towards Obsidian Dome. 0.3 mi. The road to the right is the return from Wilson Butte. You may start the loop here, or at the campground ahead. Two roads head off to the left (south). Continue straight ahead. 0.7 mi. Road to left goes south towards Obsidian Dome. 0.8 mi. Road to the right. Climb up a little canyon. 0.9 mi. Short section of pavement starts. Sign: *Hartley Springs Campground 1 mile to the right. Obsidian Dome 1/2 mile to the left. Upper Glass Creek 2 miles.* Go right, steeply uphill on a paved road to the campground. Pavement ends at 1.1 mi., at top of hill. Back on dirt in small pine forest. Still climbing on sandy road which levels off at mile 1.4. Hartley Springs Campground at 1.6 mi. among tall trees. The campground is located in a large, flat open area, and roads head in many directions throughout the campground. This is a near-perfect, remote campsite for a group of

mountain bikers. 2.2 mi. Leave campground proper, headed northeast. Pick up a road that goes downhill at the north end of the campground; this is the well graded road blocked by a log. At 3.6 mi., you hit the main road that comes downhill out of the campground. Turn left and follow it downhill out of the campground. 4.5 mi. Intersection of road marked 2S81 that heads back northwest. Continue downhill on the main road. Guide north, and you come out at Highway 395 at mile4.9. Head back to 2S22 and take the small road heading through the saddle toward the butte. 5.3 mi. Division. Take the right fork. Not too well used, but rideable. Go uphill fairly steeply at 5.5 mi. Come onto a better road at 5.6.mi. You should be just to the northwest of the butte and leveling out. 5.7 mi. If you want to climb the butte, it's just several hundred yards to the left. 5.9 mi. Blue diamonds in the trees. At 6.7 mi.,you exit into a big meadow. Turn right. 6.8 mi. You reach the main road back to Hartley Springs Campground and turn right.

Obsidian Dome to Glass Creek   Map # 7

Instead of taking 2S10 to Hartley Springs Campground, take 2S79 to Obsidian Dome, the dirt road that heads uphill to the southwest from the bottom of the paved section south of the campground. A little road leads off to Obsidian Dome parking area, 50 ft. to the left. Continue straight ahead. Pass 2S78 which goes off to the right. Continue on the main road to the left. At the next junction, go left to a green gate and walk up a bulldozed trail into the dome itself. Fumerole activity which was active after the 1980 earthquakes, is quiet now. Note the wild and wooly appearance of this place with a background of rocks brightly colored: dark grey, black, pink,and yellow. Notice also that a few tall trees (one cedar and several jeffrey pine) have been able to root and grow here. Nice view of Lava Dome , due west. Looking south and west , you get a terrific idea of the chaos involved when these craters erupted and of the range of volcanic formations: some of the rock is pinkish, others range from red to grey to black to yellow; some of the rocks are quite porous; others are pure glass. Drop back to the main road west of Obsidian Dome, and head gently downhill to the south, around the western side of the dome. Where the road branches, turn left and climb to a primitive campsite where the road peters out. You are now at the southwest corner of Obsidian Dome. Take a little jeep road that continues steeply down to the south side of the dome, then turns easterly. There is a primitive campsite, here, about 50 yards above the creek. There is no trail down to the creek. Follow the rough road to the east, climbing about 75 feet to a crest. At this crest, there is a flat area at the extreme southern edge of the main Obsidian Dome, and there are several primitive campsites here. 200 yards farther east, a trail heads southwest. Go northeast. In a few hundred yards, a trail goes back north to complete the circling of Obsidian Dome. To head south for Glass Creek Campground, follow the main road easterly downhill. One quarter mile farther, the road forks. Take the south fork along the ridge where, in 0.6 mi., you come to a power line not far from Highway 395. Turn right and parallel 395 steeply downhill about 1/2 mile to the point where it enters the Glass Creek Campground area. From here, you can bail out to 395 a short distance to the east, or you can continue on dirt roads all the way to Mammoth Lakes.

Hartley Springs High Loop   Map #7
Water: In the campgrounds.
Level of Difficulty: Moderate.
Elevation: 8400 ft. to 9000 ft.

This is an excellent quiet route of moderate difficulty with fine views. The variety of trees along the upper road is one of the most outstanding east of the Sierra Crest. From either the cutoff road leading uphill from the south side of Hartley Springs Campground, or from the Obsidian Dome Road road a short distance west, take the upper road contouring to the north. The road is carved out of the edge of the cliff and you can look back to Obsidian Dome and clear across the valley to 395. This is a nice easy-going road. At the next road divide, go left continuing to contour uphill heading north till you come to the Hartley Springs. The road climbs for about 1/2 mile with fine views of Wilson Butte. This is a beautiful route with wild lupine in season, and the numbers and diversity of trees make this a pleasure for tree lovers. Cross a sandy wash and flat area surrounded by hills on three sides. (A lot of downed trees in this area.) Cross through a dry meadow and a low saddle and start downhill. You are just south of peak 9048. Take the lower road which seems to be more well used. After a drop down, you start a short climb up, going west. At the high saddle, start down to a small meadow with great caution. The north side is steep and sandy in spots. From the saddle you can see red snow-capped mountains to the northwest. In a short distance, you come to a U-turn in the road; there's a green radio transmission reflector on the ridge and a beautiful view of June Lake below. Walk out underneath the tower to look down into June Lake, the campgrounds, the lake to the west of it and the mountains behind Rush Creek. Looking towards Mono Lake, you can see Paoha and Negit Islands in the middle of the lake. Contour down to the east through another stand of pines. The road you just came off is marked 2S78 at this point. The road to the right is marked 2S48. On the topo map, 2S48 is not shown as coming through to the campground; however, this is an excellent and interesting route. Turn right (south), passing a woodcutting area, and continue contouring below the ridge that's now to your right. Note: The road is not graded, but initially, the going is easy. In about 1/2 mile you climb a jeep trail about 100 ft. which leads to the end of the two lane road, where it becomes more or less a horse trail and continues to climb this ridge in a southwesterly direction for several hundred feet. Small trees, 4 to 5 feet high, grow in the center of the trail, but it's passable by bike. As the trail peaks out, once again you have great views to the east. As you drop down, you again pick up a dirt road, and within 3/4 mile, you're back to the starting point at Hartley Springs Campround.

Deadman Creek Headwaters/Trail to June Lake   Map #7
Water: At campgrounds and from streams en route.
Level of Difficulty: Lower section – moderate; upper section – strenuous.
Elevation: 7500 ft. to 9500 ft. and return.

This route follows a well maintained dirt road to the very headwaters of the Owens River. It is a memorable experience; the trees are lush, the Sierra Crest impressive. An excellent half, or full day's trip. Turn west off Highway 395 onto 2S01, the road

to the Deadman Creek area. Sign on right says: *Crestview Work Center 1 1/2; Deadman Campground 2 1/4; Deadman Group Campground 2 1/4* and you notice ahead to the left Mammoth Mountain,and directly ahead the Sierra Crest. Continue along the dirt road in a westerly direction. Outcroppings of hard rock on both right and left stem from volcanic activity. 1.2 mi. Y-intersection. Continue on the wide road to the left. The right fork heads to the Forest Service Work Center. 2.7 mi. The turnoff to the left goes to Lower Deadman Creek Campground. Cross the creek and at 3 miles, pass Upper Deadman Campground. Continue straight ahead on the gravel road. At 3.4 mi., a road sign warns: *Narrow road; falling rock*. The road climbs up and around the edge of a dome and follows the north side of the creek; there's another obsidian dome on the south side. As it drops down into a large flat area, the road to the left goes down to the creek and becomes 3S22 the road which heads back to Inyo Craters. (The road to the right dead-ends in a short distance.)
4.2 mi. Continue straight, a fast-going gentle climb. 4.9 mi. A little road goes to the left in the forest. This is a lovely area of mixed conifers and pine. Steep edge to the right; flat off to the left. Several primitive campsites between here and the creek. 5.4 mi. As you round the steep ridge on the right, you start to bear a little more north of west. You can see two peaks in front of you, Two Teats and San Joaquin Mountain. 5.5 mi. Several roads go to the edge of the creek where you can find primitive campsites among the aspens. At this point, you're going almost due north, and you can see the crest of the Sierra about 2 miles due west. At 6.0 mi.Turn right to a campground with tables in a nice flat area. 6.2 mi. The road drops steeply downhill, crosses the creek, continues in a northwesterly direction and gets steeper. As soon as you gain a little more elevation you can see the lay of the land. The Two Teats are the sharper peaks to the left and the straight sharp line you see is the San Joaquin Ridge. 6.7 mi. Road to primitive campsites. Cycling becomes rougher as the road (unbladed) becomes steeper and heads north,straight uphill. It's very slow going, and at some points, you may have to walk your bike. 6.8 mi. Road to the left. Continue to keep the creek to the left as you wander even more steeply uphill. 7.0 mi. You break out into the upper bowl of the headwaters of Owens River. This is an avalanche area. During the winter of 1986, many of the trees in the area were topped at the 12 ft. level. 7.1 mi. Continue steeply uphill. At 7.3 mi., Within 150 yards, the road peters out among all the litter from the avalanche. The small trail heading off to the left is only a game trail and is very brushy. (Do not take that trail.) By carrying or pushing your bike straight up the hillside, you can gain the ridge directly ahead. From this point, the drainage drops down north into Glass Creek, and you have a good vantage point of the entire area. If you are skilled in, and prepared for, cross country travel, you can continue from here and pick up a hiking trail which comes in from the east, at the 9872 ft. knoll, 1/2 mile to the northwest. From here, the trail goes north past Yost Lake and comes out at June Lake.

From this point on, the trip to June Lake should be taken only with adequate preparation and the latest local information.

CHAPTER 7

GLASS MOUNTAIN / PIZONA
Big Sand Flat to Crooked Meadow; Sentinel Meadow to Taylor Canyon; McGee Canyon to Taylor Canyon; Sawmill Meadow Loop; Adobe Valley; River Spring / Pizona Loop.

Big Sand Flat to Crooked Meadow to Taylor Canyon   Map # 8

The route across the north side of Glass Mountain will open up an area of fantastic mountain biking for you. Unfortunately, the roads are not marked with their forest service number, and the area is almost a maze of various roads and trails. However, a number of signs with arrows and mileages do help somewhat. It is best to carry the new 7.5 minute series topo maps and to check your position continuously. Many short trips and loops are possible in this area, and you'll be surprised by the springs, meadows, campsites and sizeable stands of pine trees. Because of the high elevation and the chance of getting lost, trips here should be restricted to cyclists in good shape who are self-sufficient.

Park off Highway 120 east of Mono Lake at Big Sand Flat and head southeast on 1S17. Elevation at the starting point is 7845 feet. You will be climbing to over 9000 ft. At 2.4 mi., a road on the right goes to Pilot Springs (8700 ft.), a nice campsite with relatively good water. Continue climbing to the south before turning east. Proceed through Pumice Meadow, cross a summit at 8836 ft. and drop down into Crooked Meadow, a large grassy, pumice flat. Dexter Canyon heads east (don't go that way). Take the road to the southeast. You'll find several picnicking areas and primitive campsites along the margin of the meadow. There is substantial water flowing in the meadow, however, because this is cattle country, the water should be considered suspect. Continue first south, then southeast, on 1S04 as you approach the shoulder of mighty Glass Mountain. When you come out onto the western side of the ridge, McLaughlin Spring is just 150 yards below you with good water at the spring, itself. Follow the ridge to a tree area where the road turns northeast. To your right is the west end of Sentinal Meadow Research Natural Area, and you are now at Sentinal Meadow Junction (9110 ft.) The road is signed: *Wet Meadow 2 miles, Taylor Canyon Spring 10 miles, State Highway 120 16 miles ahead.* This is the high point of the loop, and you can retrace your route to Big Sand Flat or continue to Highway 120 at the bottom of Taylor Canyon. To continue east, drop down to Wet Meadow (many obsidian chips), continue northeast, and as you drop out of the timber falling area you'll have a good view of Adobe Valley all the way to River Springs. At approximately 18 miles from Big Sand Flat, you go sharply downhill and drop into Taylor Canyon. Just below the head of the canyon, in about 1/2 mile, you pass Taylor Canyon Spring (7,500 ft.). There is good, clear, cold water at the spring about 50 yards south of the road sign. From here, it's a very easy ride down the canyon to Highway 120.

McGee Canyon to Taylor Canyon   Map # 8

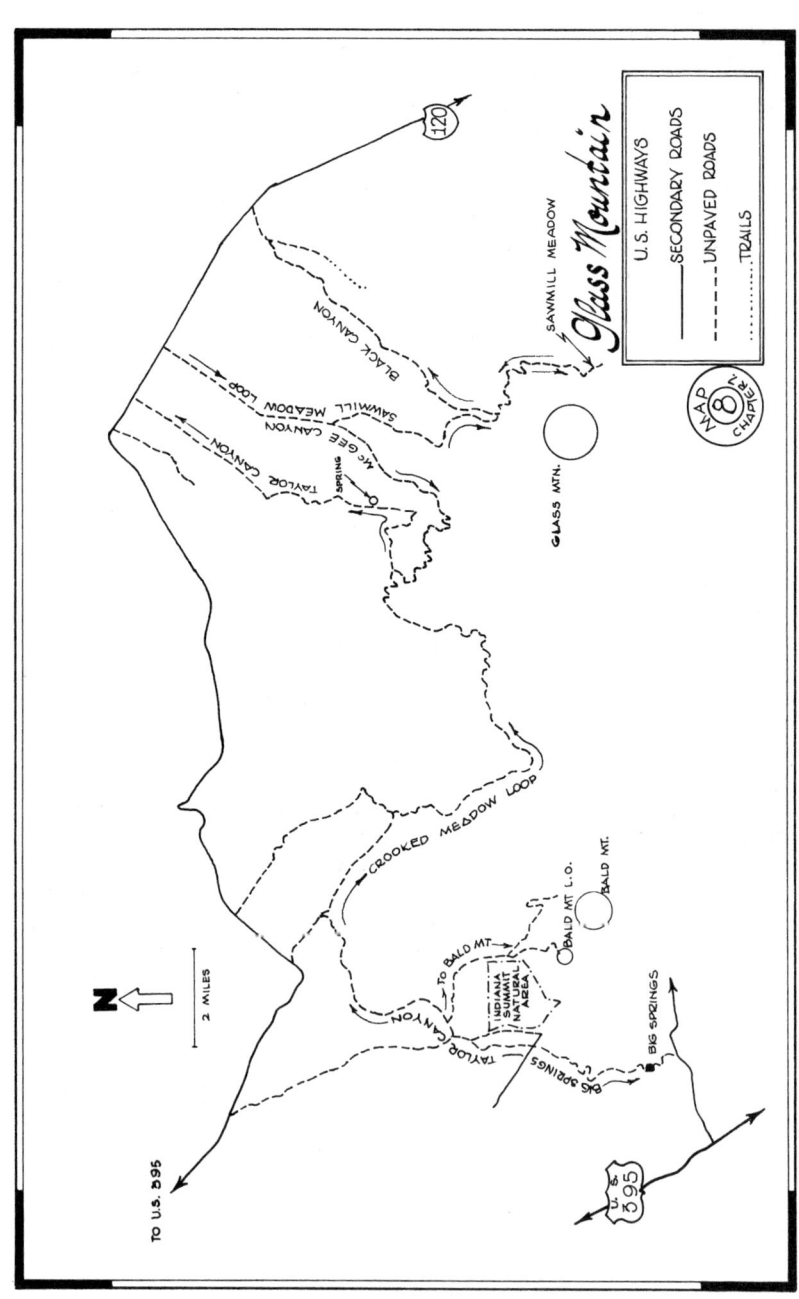

This relatively easy loop of 16 plus miles will introduce you to the north side of Glass Mountain. You leave Highway 120 at the foot of McGee Canyon and return in Taylor Canyon, the next canyon west. 0.0 mi. Set odometer and start up a wide dirt road heading almost directly for Glass Mountain. 4.1 mi. Intersection with 1S16 on left which goes to Sawmill Meadows. Go straight up McGee Canyon on 1S90. 6.5 mi. Small jeffrey pine forest. You're following the center of the canyon. 6.9 mi. The road veers right up the canyon. 7.3 mi. Major road to the left. 7.5 mi. Deep narrow canyon. Climb. 8.1 mi. After some steep switchbacks, the road levels and contours to the north. 8.3 mi. Heading west. Stay on the main road. This is an active timber-cutting area with confusing roads. 9.2 mi. Go downhill. 9.5 mi. Contour down 1S17, turn right and drop down to Taylor Canyon, passing the spring, as noted in the route above. At Highway 120, turn right for 1.5 miles to return to your starting point.

Sawmill Meadows Loop   Map # 8

For an interesting loop (strenuous because of high elevation and distance), start this ride on Highway120 at McGee Canyon, as above, and head up the canyon. 4.1 mi. 1S16, turn left. Road is signed: *Sawmill Meadow Rd. 5 mi.; Sawmill Meadow 9 mi.; Wm. McGee Canyon straight ahead; Taylor Canyon Rd. 7 mi.; Crooked Meadows 17 mi.* 6.5 mi. Water tank on right. Obsidian chips on the road sparkle in the afternoon sunlight. The road narrows as you contour up the left side of the small canyon and come into a stand of small jeffrey pine. 7.4 mi. You are now on the north shoulder of Glass Mountain. The slopes are covered with pumice and obsidian chips. 8.3 mi. Cross the creek and contour north. Primitive campsites up a jeep road. 9.0 mi. Junction of 1S01. Sign: *Black Canyon Rd. 6 mi.; Hwy 120 7 mi. straight; Dry Fork Creek 1 1/2 mi.; Sawmill Mdw. 4 mi.* Turn right. 1S01 starts downhill, curving north before crossing a canyon. 9.4 mi. Climb the ridge to the east. 10.0 mi. Primitive campsite in dry canyon meadow. The creek, here, flows from the very summit of Glass Mountain. Sign: *Sawmill Mdw. 2 1/2 mi ahead.* 10.5 mi. Leave the canyon, heading east. 11.5 mi. Ruins marked on the 7.5 min. topo map. Elevation now about 8700 ft. Glass Mountain (11,123 ft.) is only about two airline miles to your right. Notice the hand-hewn sawmill and the careful detail. The logs were put together with wooden pegs. Rotting logs in the vicinity may be as old as100 years. This structure is a testimony to the skillful, dedicated labor of the pioneers. 12.0 mi. Sign: *Sawmill Mdw 1/2 mi. on right.* Road to south crosses a creek to a nice campsite at Lower Sawmill Meadow. 13.0 mi. Sawmill Meadow (9250 ft.) Aspen and large jeffrey pine. Wooden building is marked with the names of Frank and Steve Diggins. Note that the tree stumps in this area were hand sawed; this was quite a high camp at one time. A lot of primitive campsites in the area. Note: *The water is of doubtful quality because of cattle and possible contamination.* The lodgepole pine, here, are about as big as you'll find anywhere. Notice how old the jeffrey pine look. This is a good jumping off point to climb Glass Mountain Peak, less than 2000 ft. above; and a short distance to the west. *Caution: There is soft pumice on the ridge. Do not attempt this climb unless you are skilled in remote cross country travel. Carry plenty of water.* 17.8 mi. Junction of 1S16 and 1S01. Take 1S01 to the right, a fast route leading directly downhill to

Adobe Valley. *Caution: Fast downhill following the ridge Watch your speed.* 20.4 mi. Obsidian chips all around Dry Canyon. To the east is Deep Canyon; farther on Black Canyon and Black Peak (8895 ft.). 22.8 mi. Pull off to the right to see where Black Canyon meets Dry Canyon. Look up Black Canyon and notice the jagged rock peak next to Sawmill Meadow. Notice,also, Antelope Lake across the valley to the northeast. 23.4 Caution: Road narrows abruptly to a single lane and you cross a cattle guard before it opens up again. 24.1 mi. You drop into Black Canyon. Road up Black Canyon at 25.3 mi. Corral with loud dogs and a gate. 27.2 mi. Back at Highway 120. Sign: *Sawmill Meadow Rd.* A road continues east to a stock tank and Antelope Lake.

Adobe Valley Loop   Map # 9

Turn off Highway 120 in the middle of Adobe Valley, just north of Benchmark 6650, and head northeast on 1S13, a fast, perfectly straight road that runs directly to a small building at the edge of a volcanic rock hillside. To the right, from an underground cavern, a sizeable flow of water fills a series of ponds before entering the labyrinth of shallows known as River Spring Lakes. This water is a surprise and must have been an oasis in its day. The building, here, is now neglected and decaying. Some of the writing inside the building makes interesting reading – a testimony to the struggle between ranchers who see competition for the limited grazing this area affords, and those who support the wild mustang population. Water here should be considered for emergency use only, because of heavy animal use. To take the big loop around Adobe Lake, follow the road as it makes a big arc to the north. At the intersection with the power line road, 1.9 mi. from River Spring, turn left and continue the loop in a counter-clockwise direction. Across the outlet of a wash coming in from the right (outlet of Pizona Creek) the road becomes soft and miserable. In these desolate parts, you don't want to be fooled by short distances figures, because the dryness, heat, elevation and soft road can cause slow going and large water consumption. Follow the road around Adobe Lake on the north side. At 3.3 mi., the road firms up as you approach the cliffs and veer west. Wide tires with low pressure are needed, but nothing prevents occasional piles of fine dust from fluffing up on your arrival. We recommend this trip to desert rats who thrive on conditions like these. If the going is too rough, turn back when you still can! You pass through several fences and, once again, be sure to leave them as you found them (most are closed). Before you loosen the gates, study how the curved handles work, providing leverage to help pull the barbed wire taut. Please be thoughtful and make sure the gates are secure. Sagebrush growing in the middle of the road indicates how little use this road gets; not a lot of competition for bicycles here! At mile 7.6, you reach an intersection of sorts and guide right. Pass a windmill to the left. Head west on a fairly high-speed road, watching your speed as you start downhill. At 8.7 mi. you run into the major road from the north. Turn left, heading back to Highway 120, nearly 4 miles south. As if you don't need to be told, a road sign says *Pumice area, conventional vehicles not recommended,* but how else can we push the frontiers of mountain biking? Ahead, you will see a round corral of reddish rock, about 6 ft. high and 150 ft. in diameter, part of the old Adobe Ranch. Start gently uphill, following Adobe Creek towards Dexter and

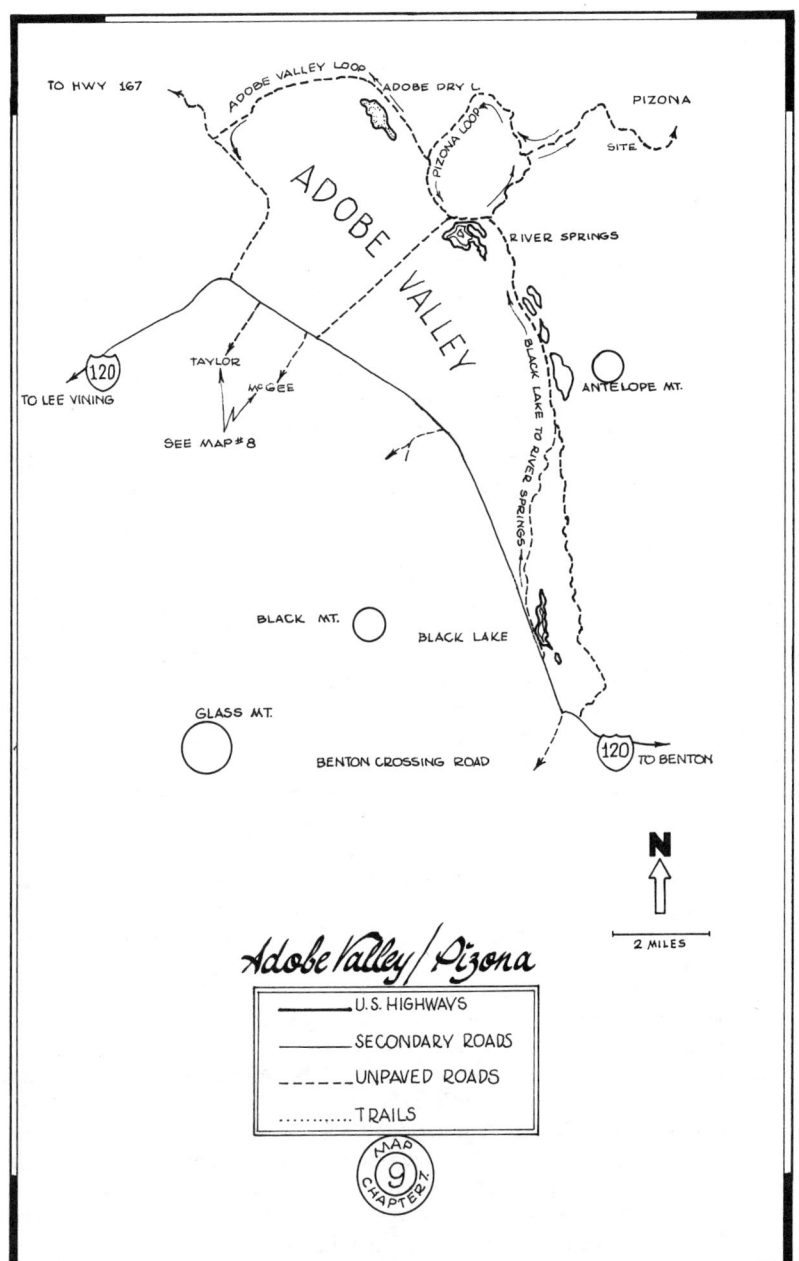

Taylor Canyons, from where it takes its source. At 13.0 miles, you reach Highway 120. Turn left to return to the starting point.

River Spring / Pizona   Map # 9

From east of Highway 120 at River Spring (6480 ft.), take the jeep road which circles to the east around an old corral before climbing steeply up the hill to the north. This route climbs over a small saddle at 6805 ft., about 1.5 miles out. The road is covered with sharp volcanic rocks, jarring to ride on, and you will curse these rocks before you have completed your ride. (The return loop, farther west, is twice as long, has some sandy spots, but on the whole, is probably easier.) After you pass the first saddle, the road drops into a small meadow and heads through a shallow pass to the east. 2.5 mi. As you drop again into a meadow, a road joins from the north. This will be the return route to River Spring. Continue to the northeast another two miles through chaparral. As the canyon starts to narrow and you approach the Pizona stream bed, you will cross a short, very sandy section. The road crosses the stream bed several times, and as the canyon narrows, you will find a number of primitive campsites, first on the willows to the left, and then farther along near the springs themselves. Continue approximately a half mile up canyon where you will come to a remarkably well preserved old rock cabin on the right near the point where seeps develop and collect in the small stream. Water quality is suspect due to cattle and wild mustangs inhabiting the region. The hills up canyon to the northeast are on the Nevada State Line.

Pizona is a remote and lonely place with a haunting feeling. The authors approached a wild mustang at close range in the stream bed by the cabin, a rare experience. The mustang, lean and scraggly, like an under-fed, sleepy, domesticated animal you'd encounter in Baja California, was browsing on watercress in the small pools of the stream bed. When he noticed us, the hair on the back of his neck stood straight up. He bolted and took off with a spirited gait, as if to prove his savage genes had nothing in common with his south-of-the-border counterpart. The sight of this graceful animal fleeing so smoothly and effortlessly was a sight to behold, not unlike a deer bounding across an alpine meadow. Surely the performance and beauty of this animal, much despised and hunted by ranchers, symbolizes the wildness of the western spirit and must someday be appreciated for its true worth.

The rock walls of Pizona Canyon are dark, almost black, and one can imagine Indians still lurking in the shadows. We hope this extraordinary place arouses your imagination as much as it does ours!

To complete your trip, backtrack to the flat area, and take the jeep trail that heads north down a narrow gully. The wash here is 10 to 15 feet deep in places, indicating that occasional flash floods occur here. There are hoof prints all over; nothing else. No fat tire tracks, no vehicle tracks, just hoof prints. As the gully opens into a flat, the road bed becomes soft and unrideable in places. You are now on road marked 1N43, and soon you can see the high tension lines which cut across the northern edge of Adobe Valley. You have left the scattered trees and are now in sagebrush. Cross under the power lines and take the firm, high speed road which curves in an arc to the south. On returning to River Springs your odometer will read just over 10 miles, but your experience may have been light years away!

CHAPTER 8

MONO LAKE / MONO CRATERS
June Lake Loop; Devil's Punch Bowl; Pumice Valley High Loop; Black Point / Mono Lake; Mono Lake Perimeter Loop

This chapter has some of the most varied and wonderful scenery you will find anywhere. No generalities can be safely made of this area and you are urged to study your routes, consult the topographic maps and read widely to get a feel for the recreational opportunities which abound here. For a good tongue-in-cheek "historical" account of life in these parts, read Mark Twain's (mis)adventures in *Roughing It*.

Mono Basin and Natural Scenic Area, Nation's first National Scenic Area, designated by Congress September 28, 1984. The legislation entrusts the management of 116,000 acres of scenic area to the Forest Service and requires protection of geologic, ecologic, cultural and scenic resources in the Basin.

The Forest Service is mandated by the scenic area legislation to provide recreational opportunites and interpretive facilities within the scenic area. A Visitors' Center is on the drawing board and other interpretive facilities and campgrounds are in the planning stages. Work on a comprehensive management plan is underway. The public is invited to participate in this process. Contact the Lee Vining Ranger Station for more information.

June Lake Loop   Map # 10

Allow half a day minimum for this loop trip. This is easy to moderate, depending on side trips, but beware of distances and climbing. The 25 mile June Lake Loop – 35 miles if you take the recommended side trip to the Tufa Reserve at South Beach – is pavement riding most of the time and will give you a good introduction to the varying features of this region, including the Mono Lake Scenic Area to the north. Recommended starting point is Oh! Ridge Vista, or the campground at the northeast end of June Lake, itself. (Note: When you approach Oh! Ridge from the east, you'll understand how the ridge got its name.)

Leave Oh! Ridge, heading east on State Route 158 to June Lake Junction on Highway 395. The route heads north on 395 toward Mono Lake. In 2.5 mi. north, go right on a dirt road, passing through the Aeolian Buttes. As you come into the alluvial fan (about 2 miles) which forms the southern end of Pumice Valley, guide left on a well-graded dirt road which takes you back to Highway 395; this will give you a feel for the entire southern end of Mono Basin. To your right are the Mono Craters, a north-south belt of volcanic craters of varying ages, the youngest of which dates to the 1400's. Crater Mountain, the highest, is 9172 ft.

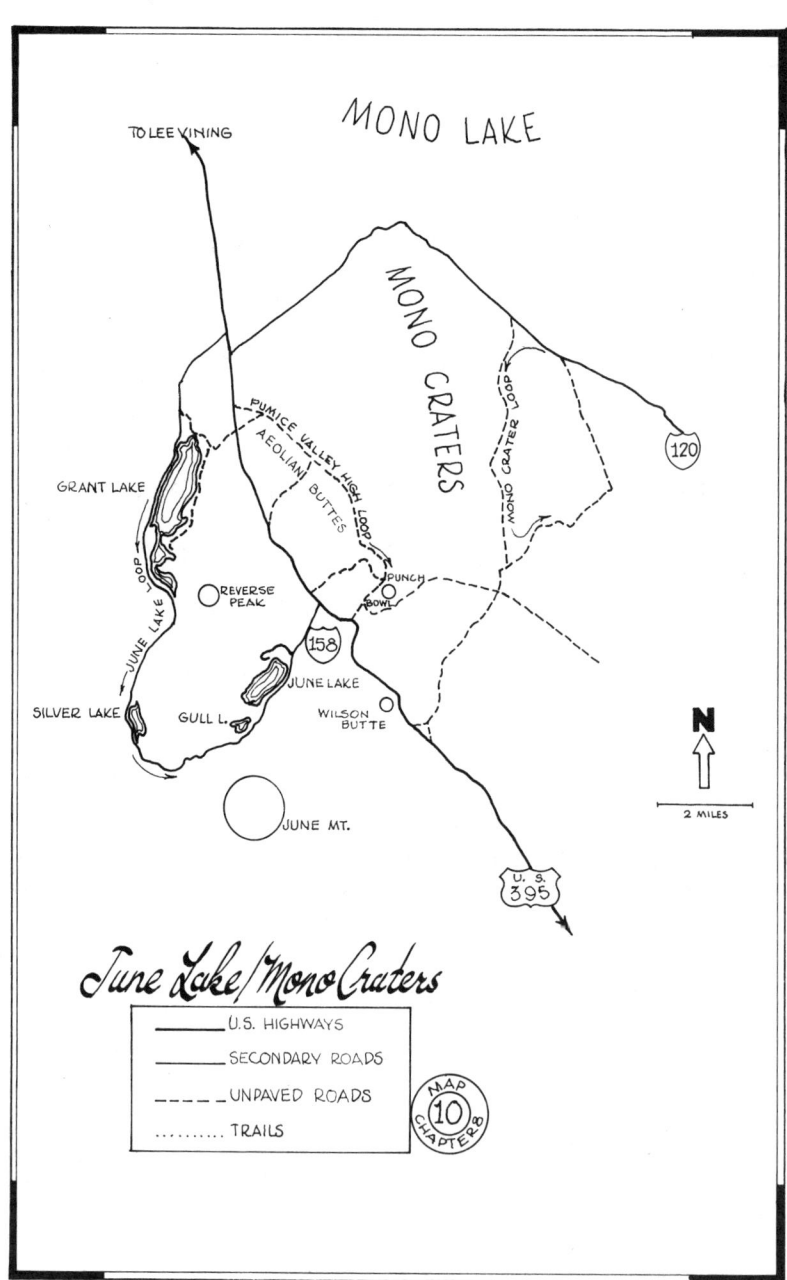

After you rejoin Highway 395 northbound,in about 1 mile, you will come to Highway 120 which heads east. Take Highway 120 to the Tufa Reserve turnoff, 5 mi. northeast on the beach at Mono Lake. Here you can inspect at close hand and read about the formation of the Tufa Towers and the highly alkaline lake waters inhabited by brine shimp – food for countless migrating gulls and birds. *(To protect new Tufa, no bikes are allowed on the interpetive walking paths or on the restricted lands below the old beach line.)* You can also visit Panum Crater (7032 ft.) – the dome to the north of Highway 120 – by turning left just before the Tufa Reserve. Continue north on Highway 395, one-half mile north of Highway 120, cross Rush Creek, and take the other end of State Route 158, heading southwest. As you climb back up towards the June Lakes, you will experience the full impact of the Sierra Crest. Grant Lake, the first in the series, is a reservoir for the Los Angeles D.W.P. As you proceed up Rush Creek, the desert environment changes to alpine, and you can see the beautiful waterfall above Silver Lake. There are many picnic and view areas as you follow Highway 158 back to the atarting point at Oh! Ridge. When you've completed the loop, you will have a good idea of the recreational opportunities in the area – biking, camping, boating , fishing, swimming and photography.

Devil's Punchbowl   Map # 10

From June Lake Junction, head south on Highway 395 for a short distance and, just after crossing under a triple power line at the Pumice Mine Rd. sign, turn left onto a paved road. Reset odometer to 0.0 mi. Stay on the paved road to 0.3 mi. where you come to 1S39 and a sign that says: *Punchbowl 1 mile to the left; Tunnel Rd. 3 1/2 miles to the left.* This is the old highway and becomes what we call the south end of Pumice Valley High Route. Turn left and go downhill to the Punchbowl. The road becomes gravel immediately. At 0.4 mi. a sign says *Danger, look out for trucks.* This is a wide well-graded road. *Caution: Many roads in the area are used by big trucks heavily laden with pumice.* At 0.5 mi., continue on down to the left. It's very sandy through here and you may have to push your bike. At 1.5 mi., climb to the Punchbowl rim and enjoy the view. If you look a couple hundred feet down into the Punchbowl, you'll see a volcanic plug of pinkish-yellow rock sticking up in the bottom. There are some good sized trees growing along the sides, so it's been quite a while since the plug was active.
You have some options at this point. You can head northwest and follow the dirt roads which meander between Mono Craters and the Aeolian Buttes, rejoining Highway 395 just below Highway 120, or you can head northeast across the sinks and meadows, winding back to connect with Highway 395, four miles south of here. The roads immediately east of here are very soft and dusty in keeping with the craters, sinks and acres of ash and pumice. If you wish to enjoy some of the remote riding east of Mono Craters, we recommend that you drive or cycle via Highway 120 to either Mono Mills site or Big Sand Flat to start your exploration. *Note: No bicycles are allowed on Mono Craters from the base to the summit.* (See Mono Craters Loops below.)

Pumice Valley High Route   Maps # 11 & 10

This relatively easy route has outstanding views of the entire Pumice Valley. You can leave the route easily at a number of points, but because there is little shade, you should carry adequate water. A few hundred yards below the Lee Vining Ranger Station on Highway 120 (Tioga Pass Road), take the dirt road which crosses Lee Vining Creek and immediately turn left (east). The right fork continues up the creek for a short distance and is a nice hike or ride. The Pumice Valley High Route is a nearly-level service road for the L.A. DWP aqueduct. It follows a well graded road which heads northeast, initially, directly for Paoha Island on Mono Lake. As you exit the canyon, you begin contouring, first east, then south, on a fast cycling road. Excellent views of the entire Mono Lake, 600 ft. below, open up like grand theatre. The road contours into the Lower Horse Meadow Canyon and you take the nearly levelroad which now overlays the aqueduct, itself. You will note the large standpipes used for inspections of the aqueduct which appear along this section of the road. The large alluvial valley in front of you is Pumice Valley with Mono Lake on the north, Mono Craters on the east, Aeolian Buttes and June Lake on the south, and the Sierra Crest on the west. This is an excellent place to get the lay of the land and lay out possible tour routes. When you are due south of Williams Butte, the road drops abruptly. *Very steep downhill (perhaps 30%). Walk your bike or use extreme caution next 200 yards.* From the bottom of the grade, you can bail out east to Highway 395, or continue paralleling the aqueduct and pass just below the outlet of Grant Lake. From here, cross Highway 395 and continue uphill on well-graded dirt roads, past Aeolian Buttes and as far as the Devil's Punch Bowl. At any number of points you can either retrace your route or head to Highway 395 for a speedy downhill return.

Mono Craters Loops   Map # 10

On the east side of Mono Craters, there is a large area covered with pine trees and crisscrossed by numerous dirt roads, long a favorite riding area for dirt motor bikes. You can make several interesting loop combinations, here, out of what seem endless choices. While most of the roads are not marked, you can find your way back to the starting point by watching the lay of the land and by knowing that the entire area drains north towards Mono Lake. While some springs with good water exist, it is best to carry plenty of water. Consult the most detailed maps you can find and/or make local inquiry, and still plan to be confused by the maze of logging roads.
Turn off Highway 395 onto Highway 120, eastbound. Reset odometer to 0.0 mi. Sign reads *Benton 46 Tufa Reserve 5; Bention Junction 46; Hwy 6 Tonapah 127; Next Services 42 miles.* 4 mi. Dirt road goes down to Panum Crater, and it's short walk to the interesting crater rim. *(No bikes allowed on walking trails; bikes are restricted to existing roads only.)*   5.0 mi. Turnoff to Tufa Reserve: Sign: *Snow not removed beyond this point.* 7 mi. Just before peaking out on this rise, you come along a steep crater. Good place to observe the obsidian and the scattered tree area; offroad it's pure pumice. 7.5 mi. At the crest you come to a remarkable area totally covered with pumice, there must have been one hell of a blowout in this canyon not

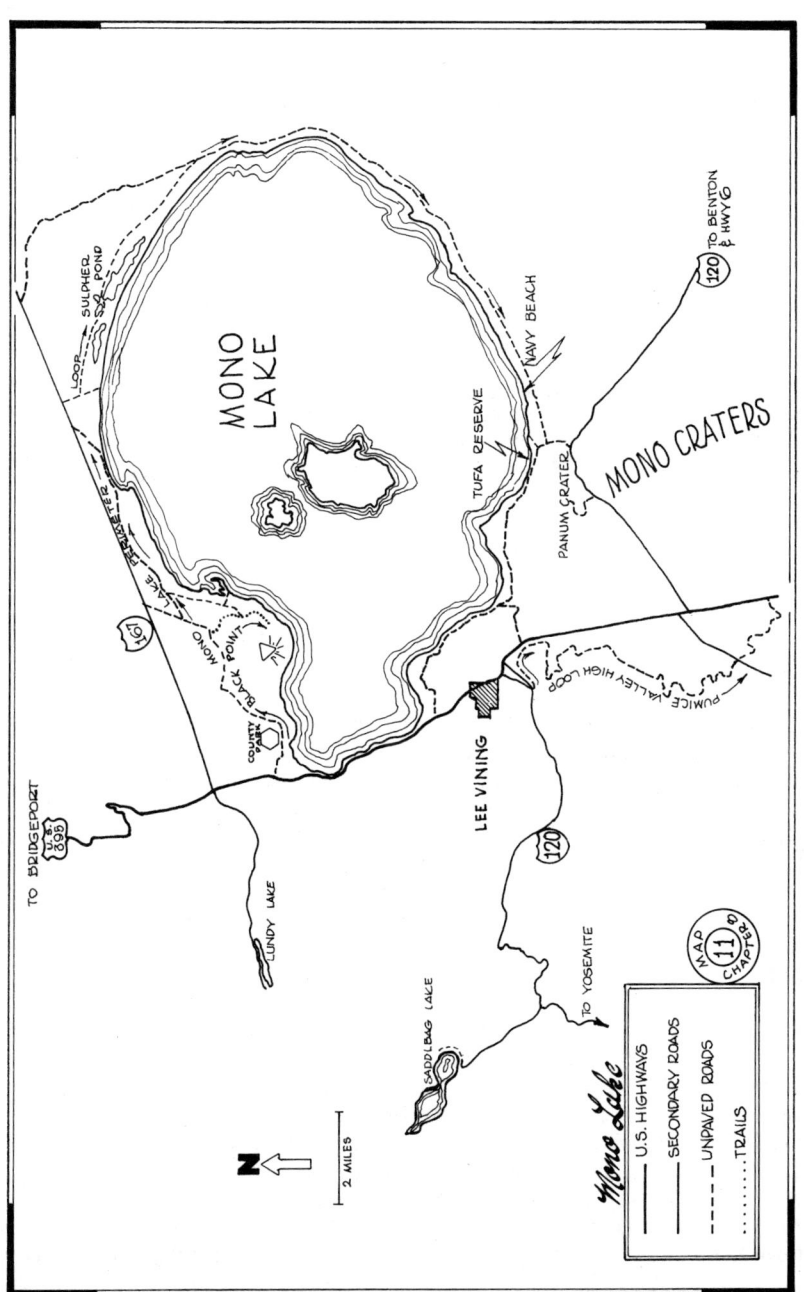

too long ago because nothing grows in this interesting place. 7.8.mi. Viewpoint 1/4 mile. Inyo National Forest Sign: *The Mono Craters are a chain of volcanic mountains. When they began to form during the ice age this basin was covered by ancient Lake Russell. Mono Lake is a remnant of Lake Russell. Initially, a series of explosions created high, bowl shaped cones of pumice. Later great domes of obsidian (volcanic glass) arose in the craters. The obsidian, as chaotic steep-sided jumbles of boulders usually overtopped with the pumice rims, advanced onto the plains. Such an advance, called a coulee, is seen here. Pumice blasted out and carried by the wind covers this valley to a depth of 20 or more feet. Beneath the pumice mantle are sediments of ice age Lake Russell.* 8.3 mi. Continue to climb through the pine forest. There's a dirt road off to the right that goes back along the Mono Craters. Fairly soft riding here, because of the pumice. This is most westerly of loop possibilities – advise you walk downhill on this road because the surface is soft.pumice. Remember, no bikes are allowed on Mono Craters from the base to the summit. 9.6 mi. Mono Mills Site: Sign: *Site of early lumber mill which supplied the lumber to build the mining town of Bodie from 1878 to 1916.* Parking spot on the left and to the right is a road. Sign: *Little Sand Flat 5; Indian Summit 6. Bald Mtn Lookout 10*. 1S13, a major road, heads to Bald Mountain Lookout with several loop trips to Highway 395 to the west. *Caution: This is a favorite offroad motorcycle area. Be careful.* 12.3 mi. As you approach Big Sand Flat on the east side of the little summit on Highway 120, the road to the right is 1S06, Indiana Summit Road. This is the main road of the many leading south. Sign *Little Sand Flat 3 1/3 miles; Indiana Summit 5, Devils Punchbowl 8; Bald Mtn. Lookout 9.* Each of these is a good potential loop trip. As you head west back to Highway 395 you near the divide which separates the Mono Basin drainage to the north from the Owens River to the south. Once again, explore this area with a sense of adventure, pratice the special considerations given in the front of this book, and consult detailed maps, being careful to keep your bearings in this interesting, but confusing forest. (At one time, we attempted to detail every trail, road and turn, but it's an impossible task.) So much logging and cutting is done in this area that up-to-date information doesn't exist. Good Luck! Remember that staying short of the divide and heading downhill takes you back to Highway 120, following the divide west eventually takes you to Highway 395, and crossing the divide just west of Indiana Summit Natural Area drops you down to the attractive Big Springs Campground, 2 miles east of Highway 395 and the Crestview Rest Area. Should you stay high and head easterly, you will eventually return to Highway 120 via one of the canyons which heads northeast from the summit of Glass Mountain, 11,123 ft.

Black Point/ Mono Lake   Map # 11

To understand and appreciate the unique qualities of Mono Basin Scenic Area, we suggest you visit the Mono Lake Visitors' Center in downtown Lee Vining where you'll find a complete selection of books, maps and brochures. You can also see slide shows and sign up for guided field trips. Short trips to the Tufa Reserve and Black Point are the basic introductions to the Mono Lake eco-system.
From a point on Highway 395, 4.3 miles north of Lee Vining, turn east dropping down to the Mono County Park, an excellent basecamp for sightseeing in this area.

Shade, water, restrooms, and a large grassy area complete with stream and picnic tables, makes this an ideal rendezvous spot. The site, leased from the City of Los Angeles, is maintained by Mono County. There is no overnight parking or camping, and the park is closed in winter. Keep in mind that no offroad vehicle use, including bicycles, is allowed within the entire Mono Scenic Area; this means no walking bikes on interpretive walking paths.
0.0 mi. Leave Highway 395, reset odometer and turn east at Mono County Park sign. Continue east on the paved road, towards Black Point, the low dome ahead to the east. 1.3 mi. Mono Lake Cemetery on the right. Pavement ends where the road crosses Mill Creek. With the heavy runoff in the spring of 1986, over 100 yards of the road was completely washed out at this point. 1.5 mi. Cross the creek, road right is signed *Keep Out*. Continue east, climbing out of the canyon. Traverse to the north of Black Point. 3.1 mi. Cross the creek and bear right to the east side of Black Point. 3.8 mi. Pass a road on the right. 3.9 mi. Pass a road on the left – this is the way to Dechambeau Ranch and the route for those riding to Bodie via Cottonwood Canyon. 5.1 mi. Pass road on the left east towards beach. (This is the Mono Lake perimeter dirt road). 5.8 mi. Parking lot end of road at Black Point. Take the 1 1/2 hour 600 ft. climb up the volcanic crater (6958 ft.). 150 yards west of the peak are several 50 ft. deep crevasses 100 yards long which you can climb down into. (Be very careful with small children.) These are interesting phenomena and well worth the extra effort. Retrace your route to return to the Mono County Park, or take the first road right (east) to continue the Mono Lake Perimeter Loop.

Mono Lake Perimeter Loop   Map # 11

From the Summit of Black Point, you can begin to get the feel for this special place. If you are intrigued by the stark natural beauty, the solitude and remoteness, and want more, consider a self-powered trip around the lake! However, before you decide, think about several serious matters before setting out. First of all, it's 35 miles – very remote and difficult miles – from Black Point around to South Tufa Beach, until you're likely to encounter another human being. Second, it is very difficult to carry enough water to make such a trip, unless the weather is ideal (cool, or rainy). Third, the trail/jeep road surface is frequently a very soft and exhausting ride and you will need to spend much time pushing your bike in a shadeless, isolated and unfamiliar environment! And fourth, unless you hit perfect weather and road conditions (such as just after or during a rain), you must plan on a multi-day trip with all of its logistics and preparation. Before you try such an undertaking, the authors suggest you try your hand at the bottomless sand trap just east of Navy Beach (south side of the lake), a couple miles of pure hell! Now for those foolish and fearless ones with more energy than sense, we give the following route information:
Setting your odometer and following the route to Black Point as outlined above, start to retrace your steps to mile 5.1 mi. where the road heads east, and begin your explorationwith the odometer now reading 6.5 miles. 7.2 mi. Pass wash with road leading right to an interesting beach area. Continue east and at 7.5 mi. take left fork. 7.7 mi. A turnaround area with old beach line and natural hot springs. 8.6 mi.

Two ponds with lots of hot spring water piped in. Road forks at end of fence. Left goes to main road; right goes to junction at 8.9 mi. which dead-ends in a deep sandtrap. Head north at intersection. 9.3 mi. Right on road east; good surface. 9.9 mi. Road soft intermittently. 10.0 mi. Enter a juniper forest. 11.7 mi. Intersection; continue east. 12.0 mi. Intersection with north-south road. Turn right to investigate rocks at the beach. Very soft going. 12.2 mi. Turnaround; very soft. 12.9 mi. Right, again, to continue east. 13.5 mi. Fence and tracks to left. 13.7 mi. Continue northeast. Road to grassy field too soft. 13.9 mi. Turn north; trail east is very soft and peters out. 14.4 mi. Intersect Highway 120 and turn east on paved road. 15.0 mi. Dirt trail on right. Double cattle guard. 16.3 mi. Take the well-graded road right (south) at highway mile marker (# 167 MNO 10^{00}). 16.4 mi. Pass a jeep road on left. 16.7 mi. Pass house on right. Take the jeep road going left (east) at this point. 17.8 mi. Deep sand. (We warned you!). 18.1 mi. Right to sulphur pond; interesting pools among sand dunes; something out of Arabian Nights. Return to fork, then east. 18.3 mi. Well casing on left. 18.8 mi. Pond on right. Road climbs sand dune east of pond. Brush covered dunes. 19.0 mi. Dry pond on right. 20.4 mi. Deep sand. Jeep trail is less frequently used beyond this point. 22.4 mi. Hard pan; fast going for a change. Dry pond. 23.3 mi. Fence line on right. Intersection road on left. 23.4 mi. Fork right. The jeep road heading back to the north is the fastest way to Highway 167 since it follows the old railroad route towards Bodie. 23.6 mi. Through gate to lake beach. 24.0 mi. Primitive campsites in the vicinity with good views of Mono Lake in the foreground and the towering Sierra behind. A very quiet and tranquil place, unless the wind is blowing! End of road at Warm Springs. Tepid spring water for emergency use only. Walk to beach. Return to road and make a decision to return to Highway 167 or commit to the perimeter road continuing south. Heading south at 25.9 mi., you come to the end of fence line of State Reserve. A jeep trail to left goes up into the hills. Continue south. 27.0 mi. Old cabin ruins on right; great view of hundreds of square miles with nothing man-made in sight. 29.4 mi. Road to the right goes to Tufa Towers. 29.9 mi. A second intersection road to right to Tufa Towers. Sagebrush six feet tall nearly hides view of lake! 30.3 mi. Road splits for several miles; deep sand. 31.0 mi. Do not take road heading uphill away from lake. It doesn't get you out of the bottomless pit sand trap ahead. Head west along lake brushline, and after an aerobic effort of first magnitude. 34.7 mi. Intersect gravel road to Navy Beach. 35.3 mi. Arrive Navy Beach. Parking area, posted *No Bikes*. After a short break, head west to 36.5 mi. and a gravel road to South Tufa Reserve. *(No bikes allowed on walking paths to the Tufa formations at the water's edge.)* From just above the parking lot, you can work your way west on good dirt roads crossing Rush Creek and coming out to Highway 395 just South of Lee Vining; or you can take the longer, but paved route, by heading south (uphill) to Highway 120 and then west to Highway 395.

CHAPTER 9

BODIE
Bodie Road to State Historic Park, Cottonwood Canyon/ Bridgeport Canyon Loop; Geiger Grade /Aurora Canyon Loop; Travertine Hot Springs; The Hot Springs

Services: Bridgeport or Lee Vining
Campgrounds: See detailed maps; primitive campsites as noted below.
Seasons: Late spring to fall, depending upon weather.

The hills to the east of Conway Summit and north of Mono Lake and the Bodie area are rich in mining history and merit serious exploring. Dirt roads in the area make for good mountain biking, and the routes and information in this chapter should provide you with what you need to start your search.
Plaques of interest in the area: Just above the Bodie turnoff on the west side of Highway 395: *1857 site of the first major gold rush to California's Eastern Slope of the Sierra Nevada.* On overlook, just south of Conway Summit : *Mono Diggings: About 1 mile N.E. of here lies Mono Diggings, the first extensive placer mining excitement east of the Sierra.*

Bodie Road to State Historic Park   Map # 12
Water: Carry a minimum of 2 qts. Water is available at the State Park.
Level of Difficulty: Moderately strenuous.
Elevation: 6834 ft.-8375 ft.

Note: Although use of developed campgrounds is recommended, you may camp on BLM land up to a 3 mile radius of Bodie State Historic Park. Fire permits are required for primitive camping. Because temperatures can vary from below freezing to 80º F. at any time of the open season, and winds may be exceedingly strong, dehydration and hypothermia can become a serious problem. Be prepared with extra clothing, water and food.
0.0 mi. Conway Summit, elevation 8138 ft., is the highest point on U. S. Highway 395 from Mexico to Canada and offers a complete view of the Mono Basin. To reach Bodie, head north for 6.2 mi. and turn right (east) on Highway 270. Sign: *Bodie 13 miles. Snow not removed beyond here. Winding road next 10 miles. Pavement ends 10 miles. No services in Bodie. Use fees collected. Cars $2. Buses $20. Through traffic no charge. Bodie State Park closed 4 PM to 9 AM.*
7.2 mi. Cross a cattle guard and continue east. 7.3 mi. Sign marks 7000 ft. elevation level. 9.1 mi. Canyon to the left. Stay on the pavement as you cross a broad grassy valley. 10.0 mi. Y in road. Bridgeport Canyon which heads right (south) is an excellent mountain bike route. *(Washed out for all vehicles, including 4 WD.)*
10.7 mi. Roads to left and right to meadows and primitive campsites. 12.0 mi. As you gain a wide saddle at 8000 ft. there are old dirt mining roads along the ridge, and Bodie Mountain is to the left (north). You're now in a treeless area. 14.0 mi.

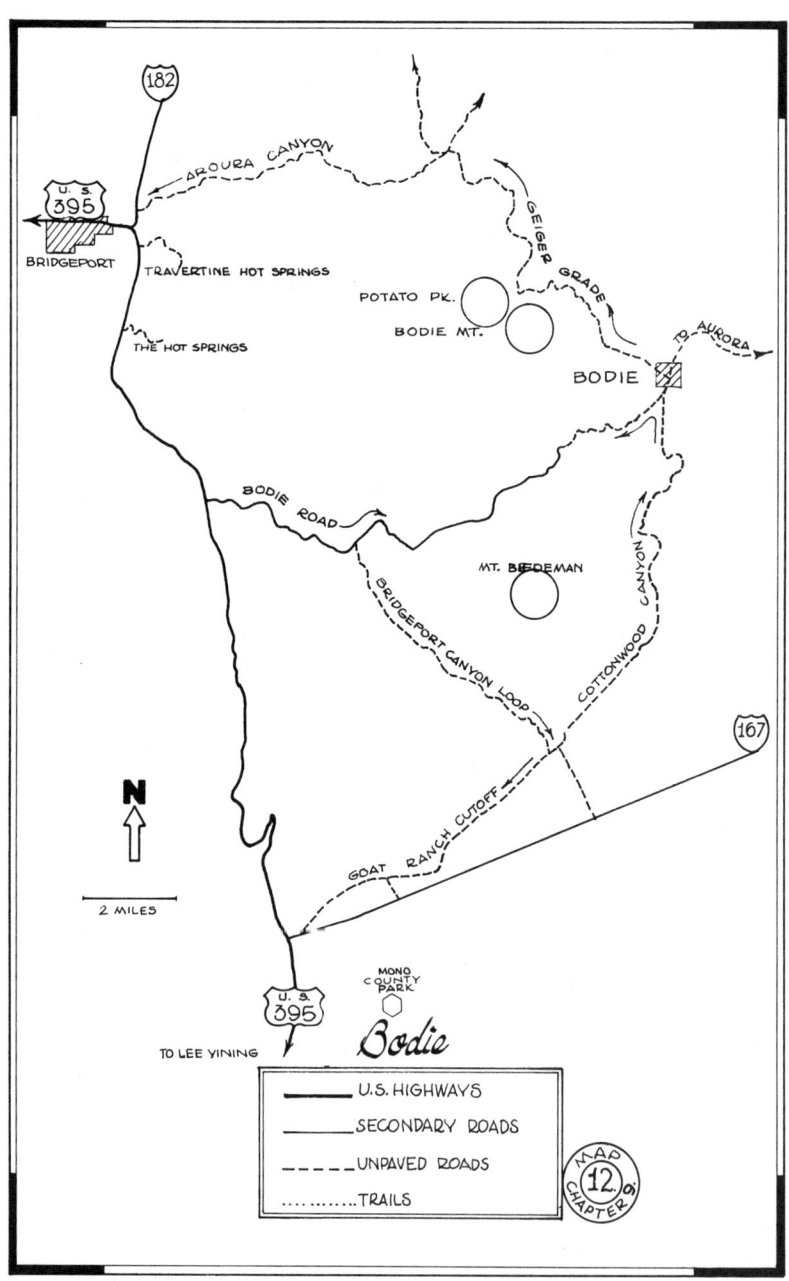

Sign: *8% grade for 1 mile.* The road continues to climb east and you now have views of distant ranges in all directions. 15.3 mi. Drop into grassy flat spot with a wind-protected primitive campsite. 15.7 mi. Hunting campsites to the left. If you want to camp near the State Park, this a good place to stay. *There is no camping allowed within the State Park. You must camp to the west on BLM land.* 15.9 mi. The pavement ends and a well-graded, wide dirt road continues east to the Park. 17.5 mi. State Park entrance and fence line at the crest of the hill with parking for a dozen cars. Cross a cattle guard and start down canyon. You can see Bodie ahead and multi-colored diggings on the hillsides. 18.4 mi. Cattle crossing. 18.5 mi. Park Gate and fee paying station. Road to the right (south) heads down Cottonwood Canyon to Mono Lake. Guide left to the parking area just northeast of the town entrance. 19.0 mi. Parking area on the north side of Bodie. *Note: Bicycles may not be ridden in Bodie proper*, so if you plan to visit the town, lock your bike in or near the parking lot, *or* walk it to the Ranger Station and ask permission to take it through town for photographing. Bodie Sign: *Gold was discovered here in 1859 by WS Bodie after whom the town was named. Once the most thriving metropolis of the Mono Country. Bodie's mines produced gold valued at more than 100 million dollars. Tough as nails. "The bad man from Bodie" still carries his guns and Bowie knife down through the pages of Western History.*
A conversation with Park Ranger Russ Guinney gave us the following details on the area: At present, all traffic in town is restricted to foot travel. Mountain bikes haven't been a problem as yet, and like other vehicles, are restricted to existing trails and roads. (No riding across meadows!) The private property outside the Park to the east is closed to public entry because of numerous mining holes and other very hazardous conditions. Homestake Mining still has active claims.
The Park encompasses about 450 acres in this valley. Water and restrooms are the only facilities and since there is no food available in the area, hikers and mountain bikers must be self-sufficient. The Park System is trying to keep Bodie in a state of "arrested decay" – as pure a ghost town as possible. Note: Although traffic is restricted to foot travel within Bodie, all *county roads* are open to public use.

Cottonwood Canyon/Bridgeport Canyon Loop.....Map # 12
Water: None along route; carry a minimum of 2 quarts
Level of Difficulty: moderate to strenuous
Elevation: 6400 ft. to 8375 ft.

Leaving Highway 395, 2.5 miles north of Mono Lake County Park, head east on Highway 167. Sign: *Hawthorne and Next Services 55 miles.* 2.1 mi. Cross a stream and pass a dirt trail heading directly toward Black Point. 2.5 mi. A well-graded road to the left heads to power lines to the north. (Note: This is an important bail-out point on the return loop if you're using the Goat Ranch Road.) 4.4 mi. A well-graded road cuts back to the southwest and to Dechambeau Ranch. 4.5 mi. Cross Rancheria Gulch and continue to descend through Mono Valley, an area of juniper, pinyon and sage. Looking to the south, you can see Negit Island and – when the lake level is low – the some-time land bridge across which predators gain access and endanger the gull rookeries. 6.6 mi. Cross a dirt road leading left and right. The right (south) road leads to the road which contours above the beach at about the 6450 ft. level. (This is the all-dirt road from the cemetary just east of Mono Lake County Park.) 7.0 mi. Sign: *Ghost town of Bodie to left 10 miles.* A wide well-graded road heads straight northeast for two miles where it's signed: *Bodie State Historical Park 11 miles. Very rough road, 1 hour travel time (by car). No services. Park open 9 AM to 7 PM. Use fees collected. Autos $2.00. Through traffic no charge. Bodie State Park is Accessible by over-snow equipment. Wheeled vehicles not advised November through April.* Reset your odometer to 0.0 mi. at 6488 ft. upon leaving Highway 167. 1.6 mi. Y in the road. The main road goes right to Cottonwood Canyon, not clearly visible at this point, and what appears to be the major canyon ahead to the northwest is actually the outlet of Bridgeport Canyon. *Caution: Bridgeport Canyon jeep trail is washed out and impassable to all vehicles, including 4 WD , at Coyote Springs 2.5 miles to the northwest.* 2.0 mi. Pass Goat Ranch to your left – elevation 6942 ft. – and continue to the northeast. 2.9 mi. A short trail leads up into the juniper trees to the north. From here, you have a good view of the beach at the east end of Mono Lake, of the Sierra, the White Mountains and Boundary Peak – marking the California-Nevada border – as well as Glass Mountain due south. 3.8 mi. Cattle guard. A dirt road on the right drops 3 miles back to Highway 167. Continue directly ahead towards Cottonwood Canyon. 4.5 mi. Stream bed. The road along this stretch is rocky but well-graded. 6.4 mi. Leave the scrubby tree area and enter a brushy area at 7500 ft. elevation. 7.5 mi. Notice the lava formations to the left as you climb steeply. 8.3 mi. The short road on the right leads to a mining prospect. In this treeless area there are nice displays of paint brush, California poppies and wild roses in the summer and early fall. 9.4 mi. Near the summit, there are numerous yellow diggings and mining propects. Pass under the power lines as you skirt the north side of Sugarloaf Peak. From here, you have great views back down Cottonwood Canyon. 9.7 mi. Summit. As the road turns north to Bodie, there is a beautiful view of the open valley ahead. 10.3 mi. Sign: *Entering Calif State Park property. You are responsible to know rules & regulations.* 10.7 mi. At the junction of Bodie Road, which enters from Highway 395 to the west, you cross a cattle guard and come to the entrance station where fees are collected and information is available. You can refill your water bottles with treated water at the park entrance below the parking lot or next to the museum in "downtown" Bodie. After you visit the ghost town, leave the parking lot at mile 11.9 mi., head west, crossing the cattle gate west of town. Bodie Road is a smooth, high speed dirt road. 12.8 mi. Crest the hill, go over a cattle guard, and marvel at the view of the Sierra. Start down into a beautiful upper meadow area. There are no trees here, but there's lush green sagebrush and grasses and you can see the snow covered peaks of the Yosemite region. As you start down towards Murphy Springs, part of Mono Lake and the more southerly Sierra peaks become visible. This is a nice high valley on the edge of a very scenic area. Climb up slightly to go around peak 8106. 14.5 mi. Beginning of pavement. Sign: *8% grade for one mile.* As you drop down into the Murphy Springs area, there's a road to the right with a nice camping area. Start climbing up canyon to a high plateau. To the right, notice the rocks from an old wagon road along the canyon bottom. 16.7 mi. A little jeep trail heads east from benchmark 80.80. 17.6 mi. A double track trail heads toward

Peak 8301. Sign: *2 miles 7% grade ahead.* You head down the steep, narrow canyon with good views continuing. 18.5 mi. Another set of tracks heads south toward a ridge. 19.0 mi. Drop into canyon bottom with juniper trees, pinyon. 19.5 mi. Meadow area. A jeep trail leads right to Blue Mining site. Nice meadow. 20.3 mi. Bridgeport Canyon turnoff: Turn left on a jeep trail which parallels the Bodie Road for about 100 yards and turn south at a Y.
Reset odometer to 0.0.mi. When you turn south you cross a pretty meadow where wild iris bloom in the summer. A creek flows across the meadow, and you need either a mountain bike or a 4W drive to ford it. *(Don't drink the water.)* To the southwest there's a shack. Corral at 0.2 mi. The road follows the west side of the creek for a while, then winds south back and forth as you climb. 0.7 mi. As you cross a creek bed and climb south heading towards a low saddle, the road becomes quite rocky. 1.6 mi. Near the summit, a jeep trail heads right (west) into the hills where there's a spring. (Treat all water from springs in this area.) 1.7 mi. Good camping spot off to the right. 7662 ft. About 75 yards from the trail, there is a mining claim marker, and a little road goes west towards an area of trees. As you hit the crest, you can see Mono Lake and the White Mountains. 3.0 mi. Continue down the narrowing canyon through a brushy area where wild rose bushes compete with the road. From here, you can see Boundary Peak. There is good camping in the meadow, but you may find yourself sharing space with sheepherders and their flocks. 3.4 mi. The jeep tracks stop here and, at 4.2 mi.,there's a 3-4 ft. drop into the ravine where the road is washed out. You have to carry your bike across the ravine and pick up the trail east of the stream bed where the canyon starts to narrow. Lack of vehicle traffic has allowed the brush to take over, so from here on until the canyon opens up, it's just you and the bushes. Easy downhill cycling another 1.5 mi. to where canyon opens up just above, and west of, Goat Ranch. To return to Highway 395, take either of the two roads that head west paralleling the power lines. Although both are scenic and private, they can be sandy in places and exhausting in warm weather. Take Highway 167 west for the fastest return to 395.

Geiger Grade/Aurora Canyon Loop   Map # 12
Water: Refill at Bodie State Park. Do not drink from springs in this canyon which may be contaminated by mining operations. (Cyanide and arsenic are present in the soil.)
Level of Difficulty: Strenuous.
Elevation: 8000 ft. to 9000 ft. to 6500 ft.

At the north side of Bodie, above the parking lot, the dirt road heading east is signed: *Aurora 18 straight ahead; Hawthorne 41 straight ahead.*
The ride to Aurora is said to be a good one on a rough road with many potholes. It's downhill all the way, so be prepared for a long climb back to Bodie. The rangers at Bodie recommend carrying 6-8 pints of water and avoid the heat of midday.
Reset odometer to 0.0 mi. To take the Geiger Grade Road, turn north and climb towards Bodie Peak. (No sign identifies the Geiger Grade Road which is perpendicular to the Aurora Road.) Immediately after you cross a cattle guard, you pass a sign: *Rough road. Travel at your own risk.* Bodie Peak, 10,195 ft. is to your left as you contour down through an open saddle. The road is rocky and grassy in

some spots, so watch your downhill speed. 2.3 mi. *Sage Grouse and Antelope Habitat Improvement Project.* The road to the west leads to Bodie Peak where you have an outstanding view in all directions. 3.0 mi. The road turns westerly towards Potato Peak. 3.5 mi. Rocky road here. Primitive campsite to the right in a very quiet area. A road to the west climbs the saddle next to Potato Peak. 4.3 mi. You gain the head of the canyon and contour to the north. There are primitive campsites and trails in the vicinity. 6.0 mi. You're on the ridge now, and if you look left and down, you can see the pipeline grade for Old Bodie's water supply. Road to the right leads to Rough Creek. From here, there's nothing man-made in sight and the views you have of the Nevada peaks to the east and the Sweetwater Mountains to the north are outstanding! Dropping down, you come to a broad shallow valley with an almost glaciated surface where you'll see glacier erratic rocks lying about. A near-year-around spring from here provided additional water for Bodie's development, and is one of the headwaters for Rough Creek. Nice meadow with primitive campsite. A road left climbs the upper canyon, to the headwall on the north side of Potato Peak, 10,236 ft., which appears as a teat with a volcanic nipple. 6.7 mi. A weathered aspen grove and springs. 7.1 mi. A well-graded road heads due east to the Paramount Mine. This is a windy, exposed area. As you head northwesterly on the high speed road, Bridgeport Reservoir and the Sierra come into view. 7.5 mi. Cattle guard. Head west. Good views in all directions. 8.7 mi. Saddle and road junction with Aurora Canyon. Sign painted on rock: *Masonic left 7 mi. Bridgeport left. Bodie back 7 mi.* Road to the north heads for Masonic Mountain, 9217 ft., in Nevada. Continue towards Bridgeport by heading downhill due west, passing a pond on your left. 9.1 mi. Cattle crossing. The road drops steeply downhill. Watch for rough and muddy conditions caused by small springs. 9.7 mi. Primitive campsite with a fire ring in the first aspen grove to your left. 11.1 mi. Cross a stream. Sign: *Narrow cattle guard.* 13.9 mi. Notice the terraces to your left which were caused by mining activity. 14.6 mi. Cattle guard. 15.1 mi. The canyon opens out onto a fan; Bridgeport is visible ahead.

15.3 mi. Road to the left is signed: *D & B Enterprises. Private Mill Site. Mercury Health Hazard.* Looking across the valley to the north, you can see the canyon which leads through Devil's Gate and the Sweetwater Mountains to the right. 15.8 mi. Bridgeport Ballpark and Sagebrush Road. Continue downhill and guide to the left to intercept Highway 395 at 16.7 mi. on the south side of Bridgeport.

Travertine Hot Springs   Map # 12
Water: None that's cold and tasty enough to drink.
Level of Difficulty: easy 2 miles round-trip.
Elevation: 6550 ft.

1/4 mile to the north of the USFS Ranger Station on Highway 395, just south of Bridgeport, a graded dirt road turns east at the 6516 ft. benchmark, and climbs uphill, circling to the right, for about a mile. The springs are at the end of the road behind the colored rocks you can see to the east. The natural Hot Springs are a series of pools of varying sizes and temperatures. The first is a metal tub, two feet deep with a very warm temperature – about 110-115 degrees F. Take the little road to the right (west) about 100 yards and you'll come to a series of four pools fed by a spring which descends a small ridge. You can take your pick of temperatures and sizes of pools, here, and as you bask in the warm water you have a fantastic view of the Sierra to the north and west. The colored rock you see here is travertine bacon rind marble, said to occur in only three places in the world. Although it has very low commercial value, it is beautiful to look at.

Please see that this area is at least as clean as you found it. Although "Caretaker" Ron Brown helps keep the area clean, please do your part and carry out your own trash, as well as that of others who are less caring – there is no trash collection here.

The Hot Springs   Map # 12
Water: Carry your own
Level of Difficulty: Easy, 4 mile round-trip.
Elevation: 6600 ft.

0.0 mi. From the Bridgeport Ranger Station go south. At the two cement forms at 1.0 mi., turn east off Highway 395 onto an unmarked dirt road. Go through the gate (closing it after yourself) and head east through a grassy, dusty canyon towards the foothills. 1.6 mi. Steep hill. The road divides and rejoins at the top. 2.0 mi. On the plateau, there are two large fumaroles with pools about 10-15 feet across with bubbles rising to the surface. Water temperature is only moderately warm but it's quite deep. You have a great view of the Sierra from here, and you can camp at a primitive campsite, if you wish. *Note*: This area is clean. Help keep it that way!

CHAPTER 10

BRIDGEPORT / TOIYABE NATIONAL FOREST
Virginia Lakes Road; Sinnamon Meadow Loop; Buckeye Hot Springs Loop; Twin Lakes to Summers Meadow Loop; Fremont-Carson Route; Rodriguez Flat

Services: Bridgeport or Walker; resorts at Virginia and Twin Lakes
Campgrounds: Many (see detailed maps), also primitive camping spots..
Seasons: Late spring to fall, depending upon weather.

Virginia Lakes Road   Map # 13
Water: Available at campgrounds and resorts.
Level of Difficulty: Steep-going on 6 miles of good paved road
Elevation: 8138 to 9750 ft.

The Virginia Lakes Basin sits on the eastern border of the Hoover Wilderness in a beautiful deep canyon. Within an hour's hiking distance from the end of the road you will find eleven lakes surrounded by jagged peaks towering above you. You can ride your bike to the end of the road at elevation 9750 ft. However, to enter the Wilderness you must leave your bike and continue on foot – a trip well worth the effort. Permits are required for foot travel. Call ahead to the Toiyabe National Forest Office in Bridgeport. The Bridgeport Valley, like the Walker River area is high elevation, remote with much solitude. Mountain bikes are new here, and there is a lot to explore and report on. The USFS people at Bridgeport are very helpful; check with them for some excellent recommendations.

0.0 mi. Turn west off highway 395 at Conway Summit 8138 ft., 53 mi. north of Tom's Place or 12 mi. south of Bridgeport. (There is a pay telephone here.) The Virginia Lakes basin is due west on the paved road. 1.6 mi. Pass Conway Summit Heliport on the south. Continue up a sagebrush-covered open ridge. 2.4 mi. A small road drops down to the stream and follows upstream several miles. You can find shade and primitive campsites here. 2.6 mi. Cattle crossing and fence line. 4.4 mi. Dirt road to the right (the start of the Sinnamon Meadow Loop). Note the large, lateral moraine across the canyon to the south. 4.8 mi. Virginia Lakes Pack Station. Nice meadow to the south. 4.9 mi. Notice the avalanche area on the south slope of the canyon. In 1986, thousands of trees were felled, denuding an area nearly two miles long and 1/4 mile wide. The avalanche crossed the canyon and climbed to within 100 feet of the road you're on now! 5.6 mi. End of the paved road. Continue up the dirt road to the right, to Trumbull Lake Campground and trailhead parking. Take time for picnicking and sightseeing in the area, or secure your bike and head for one of the nearby lakes on foot. (Reminder: Bikes are not permitted in the Wilderness and Permits are required for hiking on trails.) Note the colorful rocks – reds, greys and blacks – on the canyon walls. For an excellent downhill run return to the road just below the Virginia Lakes Pack Station and head north.

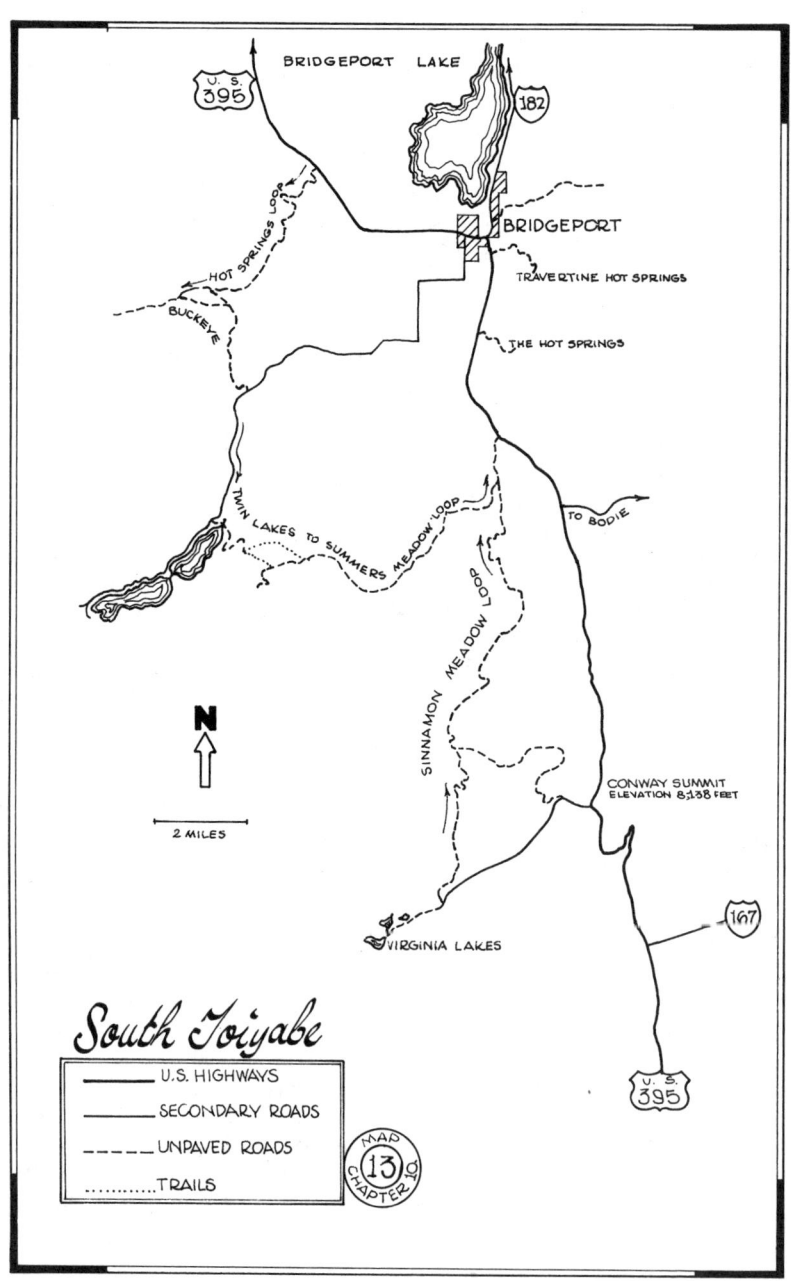

Sinnamon Meadow Loop   Map # 13
Water: none; carry your own supplies.
Level of Difficulty: 12 miles of easy downhill dirt road, and 13 miles of uphill pavement back to the starting point. Caution extreme elevation.
Elevation: 9200 to 6700 ft. and back to 9200 ft.

0.0 mi. Start on the unmarked dirt road to the north at 4.4 miles above Highway 395 (just below the Virginia Lakes Pack Station), contour to the north on the hill below the grey rock ridge. This single lane dirt road is graded and bladed. 0.4 mi. Small deep forest of lodgepole pine. 0.7 mi. Climb the ridge and enter a small forested area. Note the twisted and multi-colored double snag which resembles a witch threatening passers-by.
0.8 mi. You peak out and start downhill, passing through shaded areas and primitive campsites. 1.2 mi. Break out of the lodgepole forest and continue to contour to the north in grasslands with tremendous views of Bodie Mountain 10,195 ft. to the northeast. Take the lower, more frequently travelled road. (The road left goes to Dunderberg Mill, private property.) 1.9 mi. Several groves of aspen. Note the bending of the aspen trees, caused by heavy snowloading. 2.2 mi. Excellent views to the north, south and east. Sinnamon Meadow lies directly below you. Use caution on the fast downhill run. 2.9 mi. Cairn on the right marks a jeep road to a bald dome – perhaps an Indian observation point at one time. An unbladed jeep road to the south heads back to Virginia Lakes Road. 3.3 mi. Interesting deep forest of lodgepole and aspen forms a "black forest." Fast route, here. 3.9 mi. Grassy meadow. 4.4 mi. Bottom of Dunderberg Canyon. To the left, primitive campsites with fire rings. Road #178 – the Dunderberg Mill Road – meets the main road at this point. A trail follows the stream downhill. 5.0. mi. Fence line and cattle crossing. Road heads east. 5.6 mi. Jeep trail to the east goes out to a rock outcropping. The road doubles back and contours down to the next ridge. 6.8 mi. Jeep trail on ridge to the left. 7.5 mi. Pass a road to the right and continue working your way around to the north where you have a view of the Bridgeport Region to the northeast. 8.4 mi. Intersection. The left fork is Green Creek cutoff. Continue downhill, heading toward Bridgeport. Pass through a small group of pinyon trees. 9.9 mi. Pass under the triple power lines. *Watch downhill speed.* 10.9 mi. Green Creek Road to the left. 11.8 mi. Cross the stream from Willow Springs and come to Highway 395. Turn right (south) to head back up to Conway Summit 9 miles via 395 and Virginia Lakes to complete the loop , or turn left (north) to continue to Bridgeport. and /or the hot springs. 15.5 mi. (heading north) Bridgeport Ranger Station, Toiyabe National Forest. Pay telephone outside: (619) 932-9972. A topo map of the entire area is displayed on the front of the building.

Buckeye Hot Springs Loop   Map # 13
Water: In Bridgeport and in campgrounds en route
Level of Difficulty: 11 miles of easy dirt; 12 miles of easy pavement.
Elevation: 6500 to 7000 ft.

Bridgeport, the Mono County Seat is located on the East Walker River. Population: 500; elevation 6545 ft. Visit the classic courthouse, park and museum.

Starting from downtown Bridgeport at 0.0 mi., head north on Highway 395 to the wooded hills northwest. At 3.3 mi., you pass a major corral and loading chute to the left. Watch for the Toiyabe National Forest sign.
3.8 mi. Take a well-graded dirt road which heads southwest, climbing just below the tree line. There are spaces here where you can park your car. Be sure to park out of the way. 4.1 mi. USFS Heliport to the left. Note that Potato Mountain appears just above and behind Bridgeport to the southeast. Follow the sign to Buckeye Creek. 4.3 mi. Cattle guard. 4.7 mi. High point on the ridge. The road contours through a pinyon forest with sweeping views of the Bridgeport Valley. Note how clearly Conway Summit appears in the distance, 20 miles due south. 5.0 mi. Junction. Jeep trail to the right. Stay on the main road which now heads south. 6.0 mi. Cross Log Cabin Creek. 6.2 mi. Cattle guard. 6.6 mi. Enter *Toiyabe National Forest.*
7.5 mi. Cattle guard. Drop below the tree line, continue west and enter Buckeye Canyon. 8.5 mi. The road drops down to the creek. Continue across the bridge to the left. (A road up the canyon goes to an improved campground. The trail up the creek leads to the Hoover Wilderness Boundary 6 miles ahead. *No bicycles!*)
To find Buckeye Hot Springs, head west from the road before you drop down to the bridge, to a flat, rocky, open area, overlooking Buckeye Creek. (Parking area for about ten cars.) Work your way west, dropping down the canyon wall to the creek bed. About 50 feet above the creek, the hot mineral water comes out of a spring and falls in a cascade to an 8 ft. diameter pool, two feet deep. The temperature of the water is about 105 º F, with smaller, cooler pools in the vicinity. To continue the loop west, drop down crossing the bridge at 9.0 mi. and follow the road which climbs to the southwest. Note that there are several good primitive campsites along the creek. Notice that the granite rocks in this area have grinding holes worn into them. Small jeffrey pine forest at this point. 9.9 mi. A .great viewing point. Cattle crossing. 10.8 mi. Cross Robinson Creek. Notice the glacier erratics in the area. 11 mi. Paved road. Sign: *Twin Lakes 2 mi. right. Bridgeport 8 mi. left.* Follow the paved road back to Bridgeport to complete the loop, or turn right to Twin Lakes.

Twin Lakes to Summers Meadow Loop   Map # 13
Water: None; carry a minimum of 3-4 pints.
Level of Difficulty: Moderate to strenuous.
Elevation: 6500 ft. to 7500 ft.

This is an excellent 15 mile ride back to Bridgeport from Twin Lakes. All the elevation gain occurs in the first mile.from the trailhead. Initially, this route traverses some remote backcountry and should be undertaken only by experienced, self-sufficient riders who are skilled in off-road navigation.
From the above intersection, 2 miles below Twin Lakes, go west past several campgrounds. The view of the Sawtooth Ridge and Matterhorn Peak, (12,264 ft.) are outstanding. 2.0. Boat landing. Approximately 300 yards to the east of the boat landing, look for a sign *N.F. Campground.* Turn south towards the lateral moraine across the outlet creek. 2.5 mi. Cross the creek and continue around to the west,

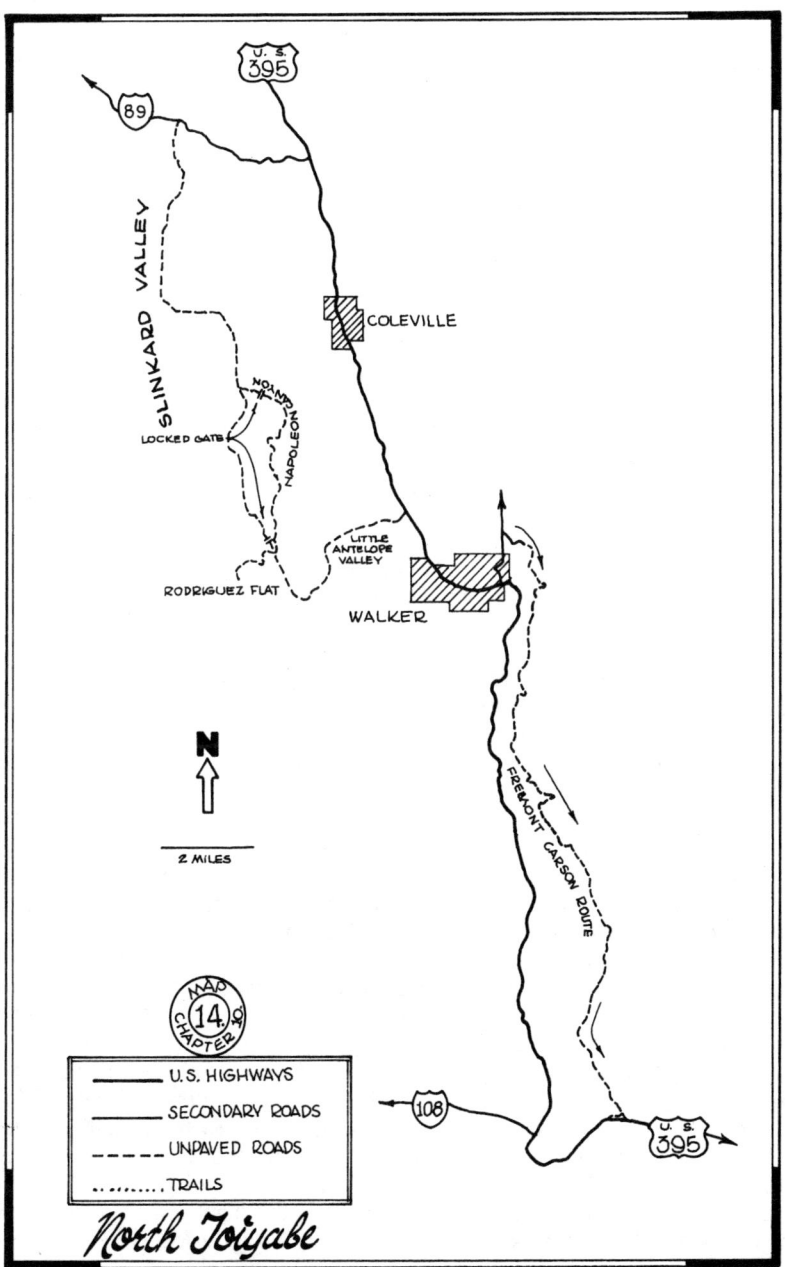

heading up the creek. 2.7mi. The trail to the left under the power lines is signed: *Summers Meadow 2 mi.; Tamarack Lake 4 mi.* There is parking for several cars in the area. The trail contours up the canyon wall to the east, gaining about 300 feet in elevation. As you come up the switchbacks from Twin Lakes and reach the summit, you will see a big pinnacle rock and a small cairn. From the cairn (small vertical pile of rocks), the regular trail turns right and continues steeply uphill on the top of the moraine ridge. Stay on the trail 1/4 mi. and leave it when the trail crosses to the south side of the ridge. You go through the middle of a sheepherder's campsite where there are two large pine trees. From this point, drop directly down to the Upper Summers Meadow, and head straight for the double pine trees standing alone in Upper Meadow. At this point, you pick up the jeep road which follows along the west side of the meadow, next to the sagebrush, and at the far end of the meadow, it joins the main road back east for about an 8 mile downhill run to Highway 395, with another 5 mile downhill to Bridgeport. From the saddle point near the cairn, you can also drop directly down to Upper Summers Meadow, head southeast and pick up a jeep trail to the meadow outlet, working your way along the eastern side. This may be a shorter route through the meadow, but a muddier trail under certain conditions. The dirt road down is USFS #144 which runs into the Green Lake Road 1.5 miles before the Highway 395 intersection. This is a very pleasant ride and will become a favorite for those wishing to get away from it all for an afternoon's ride.

Fremont-Carson Route   Map #14
Water: Carry plenty; creeks are of unknown quality
Level of Difficulty: Moderate, on good quality dirt road.
Elevation: 5500 to 7500 ft.

0.0 mi. At the south end of Walker, turn off Highway 395 north onto East Side Lane. The paved road crosses Walker River. 1.1 mi. The road cuts easterly uphill. 1.3 mi. Y in the road. Take the dirt road to the right, following the power lines, (Burcham Flat Road). Sign: *Deep Creek 6 mi. Burcham Flat 11 mi.* 2.5 mi. The road drops into a rock canyon. Contour uphill to the east of Walker River. 3.4 mi. The canyon divides. Take the left (easternmost) canyon. 4.7 mi. Continue climbing on the well-graded road. You can see Highway 395 to the west from this point. 5.6 mi. The road peaks out and drops steeply down. 6.3 mi. Road continues south, leveling out with primitive campsites in the vicinity. 7.1 mi. Drop steeply into a canyon. 7.5 mi. Cross Deep Creek Culvert. Much water; big jeffrey pines. 8.3 mi. Primitive campsite with a view of the Sierra to the southwest. 9.3 mi. You pass the trail to Cottonwood Creek, as you climb to a treeless summit. 10.0 mi. Continue southeast toward a low saddle. 11.3 mi. On the north side of a bald ridge, there are several primitive campsites. Just south, *the view of the Sierra is outstanding and is worth the whole trip.* 11.6 mi. A road to the left goes to Lobdell Lake, at the headwaters of Deep Creek. Continue south on a very fast downhill run. 13.3 mi. Cross Burcham Creek. Corral to the west. Outstanding view from the high plateau. 15.3 mi. Cross under the power lines. Sign: *Burcham flat 2 mi.; Lobdell Lake Rd. 5 mi. Deep Creek 10 mi.; Rock Creek 14 mi.* 15.8 mi. Cross the creek on Burcham Flat Road and return to Highway 395. At this point you can make a quick loop by taking 395 north back to Walker, following along the Walker River.

Rodriguez Flat   Map # 14
Water: Carry plenty; use stream water to cool off.
Level of Difficulty: Strenuous; very steep, aerobic workout.
Elevation: 5200 to 8200 ft.

The primitive campsites found in this area are used by hunters in the fall. For safety, we recommend avoiding the hunting season. Check with local authorities for dates.
From a point on Highway 395 about 3.5 miles north of the town of Walker, turn southwest at Mill Canyon Road. 0.0 mi. Within a short distance of Highway 395, you come to a Y in the road. Mill Canyon Road continues south. Take the right (west) fork which will take you through Little Antelope Valley. 0.5 mi. Sign: *Lost Cannon Creek 3 mi. left; Mill Creek 6 miles left; Rodriguez Flat 4 miles right.* 1.8 mi. Cross a cattle crossing. Head towards the high peak. The road cuts south and goes up a wooded canyon. 3.2 mi. Pass Golden Gate Mine stamping mill on the right, an impressive structure. Check it out carefully. 3.4 mi. Cross the creek. The road is very steep at this point. 3.9 mi. The road levels out a bit and crosses two streams in the forest. 4.6 mi. Contour through the fir forest. 5.1 mi. As the road turns left, jeep road # 092 goes to the right. Road # 092is an unmaintained jeep road, offering great views and complete solitude as it works its way along the ridge to Napoleon Canyon.
Caution: Napoleon Canyon Road is a non-graded, non-bladed road on a high ridge without water, but with a good view of the deep Slinkard Valley to the west. 6.6 mi. Stop to admire the view to the north before you drop steeply down into an area of very tall mountain mahogany trees. 6.8 mi. A road to the northwest goes to a small primitive campsite. Continue west downhill. 7.4 mi. Flat area with primitive campsites. No trees or water. 7.6 mi. Cross easterly and drop into Napoleon Canyon. 7.9 mi. Y in the road. The left fork leads down-canyon at 10.0 mi. to a locked gate. You are just a short distance from USFS road #203 which heads north to Highway 89 near Topaz.
Back on the main road just above the turnoff for #092 you come to #203 which has a locked gate because of a wildlife preserve. Make local inquiry because the route north out through Slinkard Valley through private property is a true classic.
To continue your aerobic workout, follow the main road as it curves to the left (south), still climbing, and within 1.5 miles you reach a summit and Rodriguez Flat. If you stayed on the main road you climbed 3000 feet in 6.5 miles! A short distance farther, you come to the Little Antelope Pack Station and the end of the road. To enhance your view of this part of the Toiyabe and the Sierra, climb the trail that heads up the ridge from the summit to the west for an excellent picnic spot. *The ride down is very steep and dangerous. Be sure to keep your bike under complete control at all times. Your brakes could easily overheat, so stop frequently and check.*

APPENDIX

National Off-Road Bicycle Association Cyclists Code

1. I will yield the right of way to other non-motorized recreationists. I realize that people judge all cyclists by my actions.

2. I will slow down and use caution when approaching or overtaking another and will make my presence known well in advance.

3. I will maintain control of my speed at all times and will approach turns in anticipation of someone around the bend.

4. I will stay on designated trails to avoid trampling native vegetation and minimize potential erosion to trails by not using muddy trails or short-cutting switchbacks.

5. I will not disturb wildlife or livestock.

6. I will not litter. I will pack out what I pack in, and pack out more than my share whenever possible.

7. I will respect public and private property, including trail use signs, no trespassing signs, and I will leave gates as I have found them.

8. I will always be self-sufficient and my destination and travel speed will be determined by my ability, my equipment, the terrain, the present and potential weather conditions.

9. I will not travel solo when bikepacking in remote areas. I will leave word of my destination and when I plan to return.

10. I will observe the practice of minimum impact bicycling by "taking only pictures and memories and leaving only waffle prints."

For further information about NORBA and to request its monthly newsletter contact NATIONAL OFF-ROAD BICYCLE ASSOCIATION, P.O. Box 1901, Chandler, Arizona, Telephone 602-961-0635.

Tools to carry with you

As Angel Rodriguez tells the story......

One day I went down and got an ice cream cone (pecan-praline), and as I walked past the bus stop towards my bike, my friend Amy got off the bus. If you knew Amy you would have to stop and talk, expecially if you saw her get off a bus. Amy rides her bike everywhere. I asked her what she was doing on the bus, and she proceeded to tell me about her theory of bike repair. It's a very simple theory: carry bus money and a bike lock. When your bike breaks down, lock it to something sturdy, take the bus home, get your car, go back to pick up the bike, and drop it off at your favorite bike shop. I was impressed. Not a spot of grease on her. Then I told her about my friend Herman.

When I first started cycling, Herman took us out on rides. Herman must have been forty or fifty at the time; hard for me to tell 'cause he still looks the same 14 years later. One day we were out riding, and my rear derailleur wasn't quite adjusted. And as it must always happen, I shifted into the spokes, tearing up my derailleur and breaking a few spokes - on the freewheel side, of course. I was ready to call Mom to come get me when Herman rolled up; he always seemed to be there when you needed him. He looked at the bike, said no problem, and unrolled his tool kit. Lo and behold, he had an extra rear derailleur, a few spokes of various lengths, a freewheel tool for every bike you could think of, plus a five-pound wrench to use on the freewheel tools. What a guy!

My conversation with Amy made me think about tool kits. Cyclists want to know, "What tools should I buy and when should I carry them?" There are two basic philosophies. One extreme says that you should maintain your bike well enough that you don't need to carry tools at all. Repair it at home, not on the road. These folks just carry phone money and have Mom come get them if something really goes wrong. The other extreme carries every possible tool to fix every possible problem on every possible bike.

My rule of thumb is that you should carry the tools to get you home from any distance you are not willing to walk.

What Ten Different Types of Cyclists Carry With Them
Adding the items as you go.

Amy	type 1	bus money and a lock
Minimalist	type 2	patch kit, tire levers, and pump
Smart Minimalist	type 3	spare tube
Smart Cyclist	type 4	basic tool kit:
		tiny vise grips (5 inch)
		pocket pro "T" wrench
		3,4,5,6 mm allens
		slot and Philips screw drivers
		8,9,10 mm sockets
		spoke wrench
		chain tool
Experienced	type 5	spare nuts, bolts and selected bearings
Touring Cyclist	type 6	spare spoke, freewheel tool, pocket vise
Smart Tourist	type 7	crank puller, spare tire, chain lube
Traveling Tourist	type 8	pedal wrench
Good Samaritan	type 9	6,7, and 8 above, for other kinds of bikes
Herman	type 10	big adjustable wrenches, bailing wire, and spare chain and freewheel and a rag to wipe your hands.

Authors' Note
A word to the wise: there are no buses in Mono County and telephones are few and far apart. You need to be your own Herman in remote situations.

Tools to carry with you
Reprinted with Permission of
Seattle Bicycle Atlas
by Carla Black and Angel Rodriguez

Angel Rodriguez has invented a series of high-tech bike tools under the Pocket Pro trade name.

First Aid

Several years ago on a mountain biking trip, I miscalculated a sharp turn on a sandy stretch of dirt road, went flying and turned my right shin into raw meat. I didn't have a first aid kit with me. Why bother? After all, I was cycling offroad, no traffic around and I planned to be gone just part of the day. When I got home, I took a shower, cleaned my wound and applied some antibiotic cream.

Three days later, Don had to carry me to the doctor. A staph infection – which took three pain-filled weeks to control – had set in.

Don't be careless, like I was. Carry and use a First Aid Kit. You can purchase a kit at bike shops or sporting goods stores, or you can make your own. For starters, we suggest the following items:

8 Bandaids 1" x 3"
6 Antiseptic Swabs or
1 oz. Hydrogen Peroxide
1 Roll Adhesive Tape
1 Moleskin 3" x 4"
1 Single-Edge Razor Blade
Sunscreen 15 SPF

8 Aspirin Tablets or Aspirin Substitute
8 Gauze Pads 3" x 3"
4 Antacid Tablets
1 Elastic Bandage
1 Needle
Waterproof Matches (in film can)
Prescription Medicine (if applicable)

For extended overnight trips add: snake bite kit; water purification tablets; non-adhering pads 2" x 3"; insect repellent, and increase quantities of compresses, gauze pads and bandaids.

The items above are available commercially in a nylon pouch under the trade name, Trekker Kit by Alpine Aid, distributed by Kangaroo Mountain Baggs and Plumline Bicycle Clothing. For a catalogue, write 3891 N. Ventura Avenue, Ventura, California, 93001.

References and Sources for Guide 2
Mammoth Lakes & Mono County

Interagency Visitor Center
Junction Highway 395 & 190
Lone Pine, California 93514

US Forest Service
White Mountain Ranger District
798 N. Main Street
Bishop, California 93514

Bureau of Land Management
873 N. Main Street, Suite 201
Bishop, California 93514

US Forest Service
Mammoth Ranger District
P.O.Box 148
Mammoth Lakes, California 93546

US Forest Service
Mono Lake Ranger District
Highway 120
Lee Vining, California 93541

US Forest Service
Toiyabe NF Ranger District
Highway 395
Bridgeport, California 93517

Bodie State Historic Park
P.O.Box 515
Bridgeport, California 93517

Devil's Post Pile National Monument
National Park Service
(619) 934-2289 (Summer only)

Mono Lake Committee
Mono Lake Office
P.O.Box 29
Lee Vining, California 93541

Browning, Peter. *Place Names of the Sierra*. Berkeley: Wilderness Press, 1986.

De Decker, Mary. *Mines of the Eastern Sierra*. Glendale: La Siesta Press, 1966.

Gaines, David & Mono Lake Committee. Mono Lake Guidebook. Lee Vining: Kutsavi Books, 1981.

Hill, Mary. *Geology of the Sierra Nevada*. Berkeley: University of California Press, 1975.

MacMahon, James A. *Deserts*. New York: Alfred A. Knopf, 1985.

Rinehart, C. Dean and Smith, Ward C. *Earthquakes and Young Volcanoes along the Eastern Sierra Nevada*. Los Altos: Genny Smith Books, 1982.

Russell, Israel C. *Quaternary History of the Mono Valley, California*. Reprinted from the 1889 U.S. Geologic Survey, Lee Vining: Artemisia, 1984.

Shelton, John S. *Geology Illustrated*. San Francisco: W.H. Freeman and Company, 1966.

Smith, Genny, Ed. *Mammoth Lakes Sierra*. Palo Alto: Genny Smith Books, 1976.

Outdoor Books from Fine Edge Productions

Mountain Biking the High Sierra

Guide 1 Owens Valley and Inyo County	$5.95
Guide 2 Mammoth Lakes and Mono County	$5.95
Guide 3 Lake Tahoe and Northern Sierra (due 12/87)	$5.95

Mountain Biking the Coast Range

Guide 4 Ventura County (due 6/87)	$5.95
Guide 5 Santa Barbara County (due 9/87)	$5.95

Exploring California's Channel Islands — $6.95
Welcome to the Channel Islands National Park
   a digital tape of environmental sounds — $6.95

Official USFS National Forest maps are available for selected areas. For a list, send a self-addressed stamped envelope.

To order any of these items see your local dealer or send a check (add sales tax and $1.50 for shipping) to:
Fine Edge Productions Route 2 Box 303 Bishop, Ca. 93514